Revisiting Henr...
Devotional Stud...

LOVE

THE GREATEST THING
IN THE WORLD

LEWIS A. DRUMMOND

kregel
PUBLICATIONS

Grand Rapids, MI 49501

Love, the Greatest Thing in the World

Published by Kregel Publications, a division of Kregel, Inc., P.O. Box 2607, Grand Rapids, MI 49501. Kregel Publications provides trusted, biblical publications for Christian growth and service. Your comments and suggestions are valued.

Unless otherwise noted, Scripture quotations are from the New American Standard Bible, © the Lockman Foundation 1960, 1962, 1963, 1968, 1971, 1972, 1973, 1975, 1977.

In Henry Drummond's work (chapter one), the King James Version is used throughout.

For more information about Kregel Publications, visit our web site at http://www.kregel.com.

Cover design: Frank Gutbrod
Book design: Nicholas G. Richardson

Library of Congress Cataloging-in-Publication Data
Drummond, Lewis A.
    Love, the greatest thing in the world / Lewis A. Drummond.
        p.   cm.
    1. Love—Religious aspects—Christianity. 2. Bible. N.T.
I Corinthians—Commentaries. I. Drummond, Henry, 1851–1897.
II. Title.
BV4639.D47   1998   241'.4—dc21   97-30340
                                                                                CIP

ISBN 0-8254-2470-4

Printed in the United States of America

1 2 3 / 04 03 02 01 00 99 98

To
the memory of
Henry Drummond
on the
centenary of his death
(1997)

Contents

Foreword

Christians all over the world will welcome this new appearance of Henry Drummond's incomparable classic, *The Greatest Thing in the World*. It is hard to believe that this remarkable little book was a fireside chat to friends in an English country house in the year 1841. Needless to say, it was the overflow of the prodigious brain and the passionate heart of a saint and scholar who had a zeal to lead people—especially students—into a deeper Christian life. As Henry Drummond points out with rare lucidity, the *summum bonum* of every moral standard is love. The apostle Paul states this with equal clarity: "Now abide faith, hope, love, these three: but the greatest of these is love" (1 Cor. 13:13 NKJV). Peter exhorts, "*Above all things*, have fervent love for one another" (1 Pet. 4:8, emphasis added); and John goes further to affirm, "God is love" (1 John 4:16).

When all is said and done, love is the heart of our Christian message. God's love in Christ not only saves us through the Cross, sanctifies us through the Spirit, but also sends us through the call of God "to a world that is dying, His perfect salvation to tell!"

Inspired by the Holy Spirit, my dear friend and colleague Dr. Lewis Drummond has remodeled this little book in a creative and ingenious manner. Like his monumental biography on C. H.

Spurgeon, written in the context of *Pilgrim's Progress*, he now has similarly structured Henry Drummond's monograph within the sequential teaching of what has become variously known as the "deeper life," the "victorious life," the "Keswick" message, and so forth. It is the message that spells out how to live in love, in the full Christian sense of the word. For over 120 years, the English Keswick Convention and similar gatherings throughout the world have followed a simple, biblical sequence of truth in promoting scriptural holiness and aggressive evangelism under the lordship of Christ. The principal doctrines are sin, sanctification, surrender, Spirit-fullness, and service. A biblical exposition of each of these truths delineates the "more excellent way" (1 Cor. 12:31) in which every Christian should walk in order to fulfill the law of love (Rom. 13:10).

I thank God for the Victorious Life movement and its impact on my life. Its teaching has deepened my love for God and others. Millions more around the world can give the same testimony. I also thank God for Dr. Lewis Drummond, who has restated this message of victorious life in *Love, the Greatest Thing in the World*. I warmly commend this book to God's people everywhere with the prayer that, once again, we all shall be known as disciples who "love one another" (1 John 3:23).

STEPHEN F. OLFORD

Introduction

For over one hundred years Henry Drummond's classic monograph on 1 Corinthians 13, *The Greatest Thing in the World*, has strengthened and blessed millions of Christians. It remains in print to the present hour and continues to minister to multitudes.

All this is logical and correct, for love—the greatest thing in the world—constitutes the heart of the Christian experience. It fulfills the Great Commandment and exemplifies God Himself: "God is love." In Drummond's exposition of the "love chapter" he asks, "What is the *summum bonum*—the supreme good?" He correctly answers with Paul's own words, "the greatest of these is love" (1 Cor. 13:13), and concludes with John's words, "Everyone that loveth is born of God" (1 John 4:7). Drummond has struck the keynote of Christianity. Little wonder his small volume has entered the realm of classic Christian literature.

But the work is now a century old. Perhaps the time has arrived to revisit this simple yet profound exposition wherein Henry Drummond laid out clearly the principle and praise of agape (God's quality of love). More relevant than a mere reprinting, however, which comprises the first chapter of this present work, an expansion of the little book could perhaps prove fruitful; the reason being, Drummond went into little detail

9

on *how* to attain that level of Christian living. One thing seems clear: Not many believers today live on the agape love plane in their daily lives even though they may realize its centrality in their Christian experience. Therefore, this revisiting of Drummond's work by another Drummond shall carry on where Henry Drummond's small volume left off and attempt to lay out in a very practical way the foundational principles of how true Christian love can be realized in daily experience.

I trust that it will not appear presumptuous to add to Drummond's classic monograph. It will always stand on its own as an excellent piece of devotional material. It could never be improved upon, only expanded, which this present work attempts to do. So on the centenary of Henry Drummond's death, it seems an appropriate time to look again at *The Greatest Thing in the World*.

Gratitude goes to those who helped make this revisiting of Henry Drummond's work a reality. To Michelle Joiner, my very able secretary, I express thanks. To Dennis Hillman of Kregel Publications, I am grateful. Dr. Stephen Olford, friend and brother in Christ, who penned the foreword, I thank very much. Above all to Henry Drummond himself who gave us his classic work, I express the gratitude of the multitudes who have been blessed, challenged, and strengthened in their Christian faith by his writing. May God use it all to His honor and glory.

LEWIS A. DRUMMOND

Prologue

A Sketch of the Life and Ministry of Henry Drummond

Look, in this town there is a man of God; he is highly respected.

1 Samuel 9:6 NIV

History records many great personalities who have come out of the Scottish-Christian context. A goodly number have made incalculable contributions to the cause of Christ. When one thinks of Scottish evangelicalism, significant names surface: John Knox, the reformer; Robert Murray McCheyne, the pastor; David Livingstone and Mary Slessor of Calabar, the missionaries; and in more recent times, great preachers such as James Stewart and Bible scholars such as William Barclay. In the nineteenth century Scotland produced a most unusual man of God who ultimately impacted many parts of the world. A professor of science, an ordained minister of the Free Church of Scotland, and a brilliant mind coupled with a devoted life to Christ, he wrote extensively, preached powerfully, ministered devotedly, and thus made his contribution to the Christian church. His name was Henry Drummond.

One hundred years ago God called Drummond to his eternal reward. And a noble reward it no doubt is. His deep devotion to Jesus Christ and his unflagging zeal in spreading the gospel of Christ made a tremendous impression on all who knew him. His life and work remain as a monument of God's grace to this day. At the centenary of his death, 1997, he continues to influence many through his writings. His dedication to win people to Christ along with his absolute commitment to propagating a mature and vital understanding of the Christian faith in the midst of the enamorment of science in his day, stands as a tribute to the integrity and zeal he so exemplified through his relatively short life. His greatest contribution, at least his most well-known contribution, *The Greatest Thing in the World*, has remained in print for over one hundred years since its writing. The small work on 1 Corinthians 13 enhances the shelves in bookstores yet today and continues to bless and challenge believers. Therefore, it seems correct at such a time to revisit Drummond's classic monograph on Christian love.

Henry Drummond was born in Sterling, Scotland, on August 17, 1851. He died at Tonbridge Wells, a beautiful small town southeast of London, on March 11, 1897. Still, in those forty-six short years, he made a most significant contribution to the Christian faith. Drummond lived through a very distinctive period in Britain—the last quarter of the nineteenth century. The full impact of Darwinism, the philosophy of Spencer that capitalized on the popularity of Darwin, and the inroads of German rationalistic theology, not to mention the tremendous explosion in science, made that quarter-century one of the most volatile and yet significant periods in the Western world.

In the last twenty-five years of the nineteenth century the spirit of the Victorian era with its distinctive religious flavor began to experience its demise; but at the same time, many of the great Victorian preachers still valiantly held forth against a barrage of humanistic attacks on the faith. Alexander Maclaren, James Wells, Joseph Parker, and, above all, Charles Haddon Spurgeon still graced the scene hoping to stem the tide of an encroaching secularism. At such a time of ferment, some able mind was sorely needed to contend for the Christian faith in light of the onslaught that had begun to attack the evangelicalism of the day. Although somewhat of a controversial figure in the thinking of some, God destined Henry Drummond to be one of those who stood in the gap, and with a great measure of success he kept many from straying away from essential biblical truth.

Henry Drummond had an inherent love for and keen interest

in the natural sciences. Even as a lad he became fascinated by the advances in that field. Much of his later ministry unfolded in a quest to help people understand that true science and a proper grasp of Christian truth do not conflict. One of his larger works, *Natural Law and the Spiritual Life*, sold well over one hundred thousand copies, not to mention many other pamphlets and small volumes on the subject that he wrote in the course of his service. His magnum opus, *The Greatest Thing in the World*, has sold over one million copies in the one hundred years since its writing. Needless to say, he wielded a capable pen.

At a very early age Henry showed promise of making a mark on his generation. After some years of study in private schools at Sterling, at the age of fifteen he secured admission in New College, the University of Edinburgh, to work on his baccalaureate degree. Drummond's father, who also bore the name Henry, served Sterling as a justice of the peace, and this no doubt contributed to an early bent in young Henry for serious study. Drummond studied long and hard at Edinburgh, and although he did not in one sense do outstanding work, his rare gifts marked him out among his classmates and demonstrated great promise.

When Drummond went to Edinburgh, the only visible signs of any vital Christian faith among the students at the University centered in a prayer meeting attended by just a mere dozen men. But Drummond's influence proved to be tremendous on New College and even to some extent on the whole university. Such was the godliness of his life.

Being brought up in a godly home, Drummond came to a living faith in the Lord Jesus Christ at an early age. He determined that he would give himself to the Christian ministry. He committed his life to serve his Lord as a minister of the gospel and was ordained in the Free Church of Scotland. After completing work at New College, Edinburgh, he studied at the Free Church Divinity Hall. During a summer term he made his way to Tübingen, Germany, for further study. He never became the pastor of a church; his ministry moved in the direction of education where he made his remarkable contribution.

Drummond's formal theological education and ordination in the Free Church of Scotland equipped him for a short term in a mission station in Malta. There, where the demands were not exceedingly pressing, he once again began to manifest that keen early interest in relating his lifelong love of science and the Christian faith. He read extensively in the general scientific field and became very conversant in the latest trends in theology. This set a distinct course for the young man of God. His goal was to demonstrate the relationship between science and religion. He deeply felt that one need not discard all the discoveries of modern science in the name of religion or vice versa. Drummond argued that God's truth stands eternal and is all-pervasive, and therefore a way can be found to resolve any supposed conflict between true science and genuine Christianity. To that end he gave much of his life.

To reflect back a short time before Drummond's formal ordination, an interesting occurrence took place that helped shape and give direction to the young ministerial student. As Drummond pondered the profound question of the Christian faith and the explosion of the natural sciences of his day, the well-known American evangelist D. L. Moody came to Edinburgh for an evangelistic crusade. A very significant event occurred there in the life of Henry Drummond.

Moody was anything but a highly educated man. He "butchered" the English language, as some Britishers said. It would seem that the sophisticated clientele of the University of Edinburgh would hardly take him seriously. Of course, many did not and thought him something of an American "country bumpkin" with no real abilities and hence no real right to preach to their scholarly community. But many of the University were deeply moved by the simple yet spiritually powerful message and ministry of Moody. Henry Drummond became one of those. Moody touched his life profoundly.

As soon as Moody had come to Edinburgh for his evangelistic mission, Drummond heard him and identified himself with him. He saw Moody as a very capable, honest, and unselfish evangelist. Henry Drummond actually spent a protracted period working with Moody in the ministry of evangelism throughout the United Kingdom.

Drummond had always nurtured a concern for the propagation of the Christian faith, but now having experienced a productive time with the great evangelist, an even deeper burden to win people to personal faith in Jesus Christ permeated his life. It is fair to say that Drummond became a most astute evangelist in his own right. He gave himself to the winning of the lost and did it with a vigor and a zeal seldom seen. He proved especially effective in the higher intellectual circles in which he lived out most of his service. As one put it, "He made himself a great speaker; he knew how to seize the critical moment, and with his modesty, his refinement, his gentle and generous nature, his manliness, and above all, his profound conviction, won for him disciples in every place he visited."[1]

After Henry Drummond completed his formal education, a wide-ranging ministry unfolded for the young man. He touched many lives for Christ in many ways. He had a magnetic personality. All who knew Drummond thought him a very attractive and winsome man. He is described by one author with these words:

> Drummond was a handsome man, such as you could not match in ten days' journey, with delicately cut features, rich auburn hair, and a certain carriage of nobility, but the distinctive and commanding feature of his face was his eye. No photograph could do it justice, and very often photographs have done it injustice, by giving the idea of

staringness. His eye was not bold or fierce; it was tender and merciful. But it had a power and hold which were little else than irresistible and almost supernatural. When you talked with Drummond, he did not look at you and out of the window alternately, as is the usual manner; he never moved his eyes, and gradually their penetrating gaze seemed to reach and encompass your soul. It was as Plato imagined it would be in the judgment; one soul was in contact with another—nothing between. No man could be double, or base, or mean, or impure before that eye. His influence, more than that of any man I have ever met, was mesmeric— which means that while other men affect their fellows by speech and example, he seized one directly by his living personality.[2]

Not only was Drummond a very captivating person in appearance, he had tremendous appeal in his entire ministry. The same biographer also said:

He was the Evangelist to thoughtful men—over women he had far less power—and his strength lay in his personality. Without anecdotes or jokes, or sensationalism or doctrine, without eloquence or passion, he moved young men at his will because his message was life, and he was its illustration. His words fell one by one with an indescribable awe and solemnity, in the style of the Gospels, and reached the secret place of the soul. Nothing more unlike the ordinary evangelistic address could be imagined: it was so sane, so persuasive, so mystical, so final. It almost followed, therefore, that he was not the ideal of a popular evangelist who has to address the multitude, and produce his effect on those who do not think. For his work, it is necessary— besides earnestness, which is taken for granted—to have a loud voice, a broad humor, a stout body, a flow of racy anecdotes, an easy negligence of connection, a spice of contempt for culture, and pledges of identification with the street in dress and accent. His hearers feel that such a man is homely and is one of themselves, and, amid laughter and tears of simple human emotion, they are moved by his speech to higher things. This kind of audience might regard Drummond with respectful admiration, but he was too fine a gentleman, they would consider, for their homespun. Place him, as he used to stand and speak, most perfectly dressed both as to body and soul, before five hundred men of good taste and fine sensibilities, or the same number of young men not yet cultured but full of intellectual ambitions and fresh enthusiasm, and no man could state the case for Christ and the soul after a more spiritual and winsome fashion. Religion is without doubt the better for the popular evangelist, although there be times when quiet folk think that he needs chastening; religion also requires in every generation one representative at least of the higher evangelism, and if any one should ask what manner of man he ought to be, the answer is to his hand—Henry Drummond.[3]

Needless to say, Henry Drummond possessed an inviting personality that captured many for Christ.

Drummond traveled widely through the years. He covered the continent of Europe, traveled to Australia, evangelized in Africa, and made a deep impression on America during three different trips. He became quite well-known in virtually all of the Western world. He ministered with D. L. Moody while in the United States. The famous evangelist invited Drummond on one occasion to speak at the prominent Northfield Bible Conference. An interesting anecdote occurred in that setting. When Moody first asked Drummond to speak at Northfield, Henry felt some reluctance to accept the evangelist's invitation. He said, "Mr.

Moody, I might not be well received because I believe that the book of Isaiah can be divided into two basic divisions; into *two* Isaiahs." (Many Old Testament scholars hold to the view that there is a 1 Isaiah and a 2 Isaiah, similar to 1 Corinthians and 2 Corinthians.) Mr. Moody immediately replied, "Don't worry about that, my friend. There are a lot of people who don't even know there is *one* Isaiah." So Drummond went to America and impacted the Bible conference tremendously with his godly and astute Bible studies.

Drummond's ministry developed through the years and took many different turns. For example, he would take groups of students to towns and villages on what he called "holiday missions." Student ministries gained a significant role during the last part of the nineteenth century. As a case in point, the well-known "Cambridge Seven" were making their lives felt in British student life. A group of seven Cambridge University students traveled over the country challenging hearers to deep devotion to Jesus Christ. One of the seven was the well-known C. T. Studd, a star on the cricket field. He later became the founder of the World Evangelization Crusade that still sends multitudes of missionaries around the world. This entire general ethos proved helpful in the developing student ministry of Henry Drummond.

At the young age of twenty-six, after completing a period of serving the Lord in various ways, Drummond became a lecturer on natural science at the Free Church College at Glasgow University in 1877. There he came under the influence of the godly pastor Marcus Dods, to whom Henry always said he owed more than to any other man. Drummond worked in a mission affiliated with Dr. Dods' church, and there he preached a series of addresses later published as *Natural Law and the Spiritual World*. This book appeared in 1883 and became an immediate best-seller in religious circles. It constituted something of the culmination of his views on the relationship of science and religion.

Drummond's position at the University of Glasgow evolved in 1884 into a full chair and professorship for the able man. As a professor challenging his students, he made one of his most important contributions to the cause of the kingdom. He held that chair for the rest of his life.

The Free Church of Scotland at the time was racked by something of an extreme conservative movement that threatened to dampen the spiritual fervor of the congregations and immerse them completely in theology alone. Drummond contributed significantly toward a resolution by injecting a spiritual balance back into the Free Church, and, as a consequence, some biographers maintained that he saved the denomination from a serious pitfall.

University life at Glasgow did not completely occupy Henry. For many years he would travel once a week from Glasgow to Edinburgh to deliver a Sunday evening message. The place where he spoke always filled, and the majority of those attending the lectures were medical students. On many occasions he gave lectures and addresses in London to political leaders, and eminent men of the time flocked to hear him. He had a unique personal touch. One biographer said that if in his studies Henry came upon some good thought, he would walk a mile to share it with a friend. Drummond was a self-giving man. In a very real sense, he exemplified the greatest thing in the world.

As perhaps can be imagined, Henry Drummond had his critics; some even accused him of theological heresy. Yet it must be said that he held tenaciously to the essential gospel of Jesus Christ. It may well be true that his main emphasis and thrust did not center on how a person can save his or her *soul* but how a person can save his or her *life*. His basic concept of salvation revolved around rising to the stature of Christ and being a participant in the simple, peaceful, loving life of the Lord. Perhaps he could have had a stronger emphasis upon the destructive power of sin, but he was such a godly man himself that he felt that the quest of the Christian life culminated in attaining godliness as seen in self-giving Christian love.

Of course, Drummond definitely saw the need of Christ's forgiveness of sins. It seems correct to say that he was not a theologian in the sense of developing a formal system of doctrine. His commitment pointed more toward helping people experience the greatest thing in the world. At the same time, it would not be correct to call him antitheological—it would probably be more proper to say that he was nontheological in the formal sense. His life and focus totally fixed itself upon the life of Jesus and how to live pleasing to Him and in aiding others in the quest to find God's peace in Jesus Christ. His heart burned to help others he knew and loved to the Lord. It has been reported of Drummond that he would at times decline an invitation to speak to a large gathering because he had made an appointment with just one person to share the message of Christ with that single needy soul. That is true self-denying love.

Henry Drummond's famous composition, *The Greatest Thing in the World*, developed in what would be a normal fashion for Drummond. In 1889 he received an invitation to bring an address to a small group at Oxford. He presented a simple essay entitled "The Greatest Thing in the World." Those who heard him immediately demanded its publication. Drummond never seemed eager to see his works go to press, but the hearers so insisted that he soon published the monograph and it became the century-old classic still loved today.

Often, those who write well do not speak well, and those who are gifted in oratory seem poor writers. But Drummond had both gifts in a marvelous, God-given fashion. Hence his popularity became all but universal. Probably the secret of his success centered in his simplicity and clearness of style. He said that every work ought to go through three steps to production. The first draft of a work should be characterized by simplicity. The second draft should be very profound. The final draft for publication or for addressing an audience should be presenting very profound things in a very simple fashion. That became his working philosophy in all his communication, written and oral. As the reader goes through his classic, *The Greatest Thing in the World*, it will become evident that this is exactly what Drummond accomplished. As one biographer put it:

> He has a certain magnetic quality, both as a writer and a speaker, but it can be analyzed. He has a style—not a style to move "the lonely rapture of lonely minds," but one which arrests the busy crowd—clear, pleasant, flowing with faint hues of poetry. He is never allusive, superior, strained; he does not condescend; he is always himself—a courteous, unaffected gentleman, with a sincere respect for his audience. He is adept in the art of translating scientific ideas into common English, and can impart the touch that redeems the familiar from platitude.[4]

In this basic matrix he composed *The Greatest Thing in the World*.

Henry Drummond's last days were fraught with severe discomfort. Early biographers tell us that he contracted a serious bone disease that left his body literally racked in pain. Perhaps he had bone cancer; it has never been determined. Regardless, he certainly spent his last months in agony. Even in the face of that anguish, however, one could always count on the same Henry Drummond. He invariably had a cheerful and encouraging word for those who would visit him. It was said of him during his last days,

> The spectacle of his long struggle with a mortal disease was something more than impressive. Those who saw him in his illness saw that, as the physical life flickered low, the spiritual energy grew. Always gentle and considerate, he became even

more careful, more tender, more thoughtful, more unselfish.
He never in any way complained. . . . It was not like death.
He lay on his couch in the drawing room and passed away in
his sleep, with the sun shining in and the birds singing in the
open window. There was no sadness or farewell.[5]

Drummond himself said, concerning the death of one of his
friends, that his friend was simply "putting by the well-worn tools
without a sigh, and expecting elsewhere better work to do."[6]
He felt the same way about himself.

Henry Drummond died at the age of forty-six in Tonbridge
Wells, England. Friends laid him to rest on a blustery March
day near his home in Sterling as the world mourned the loss of
a great man. He was a student, a thinker, a professor, but above
all a loving man of God. Bernard of Clairvaux put it well when
he wrote of such people:

> There are many
> who seek knowledge
> for the sake of knowledge:
> That is curiosity.
>
> There are others who desire
> to know in order that they
> may themselves be known:
> That is vanity.
>
> But there are some who
> seek knowledge in order to
> serve and edify others:
> And that is love.

Henry Drummond's biographer, John Watson, said, "Henry
Drummond was the most perfect Christian I have ever known

or expect to see this side of the grave." Why such a eulogy? Because he not only spoke and wrote on the subject, he exemplified in his life the greatest thing in the world.

Endnotes

1. Ian Maclaren, introduction to *The Ideal Life,* by Henry Drummond (New York: Dodd, Mead and Company, 1898), 8.
2. Ibid., 28-29.
3. Ibid., 30-31.
4. *Drummond's Addresses* (Chicago: Donohue, Henneberry & Co.), vi-vii.
5. Drummond, *The Ideal Life*, 23.
6. Ibid.

I

The Greatest Thing in the World

by Henry Drummond (1851-1897)

*But now abide faith, hope, love, these three;
but the greatest of these is love.*

1 Corinthians 13:13

Though I speak with the tongues of men and of angels, and have not love, I am become as sounding brass, or a tinkling cymbal. And though I have the gift of prophecy, and understand all mysteries, and all knowledge; and though I have all faith, so that I could remove mountains, and have not love, I am nothing. And though I bestow all my goods to feed the poor, and though I give my body to be burned, and have not love, it profiteth me nothing.

Love suffereth long, and is kind;
love envieth not;
love vaunteth not itself, is not puffed up,
doth not behave itself unseemly,
seeketh not her own,
is not easily provoked,
thinketh no evil;
rejoiceth not in iniquity, but rejoiceth in the truth;
beareth all things, believeth all things, hopeth all things, endureth all things.

Love never faileth: but whether there be prophecies, they shall fail; whether there be tongues, they shall cease; whether there be knowledge, it shall vanish away. For we know in part, and we prophesy in part. But when that which is perfect is come, then that which is in part shall be done away. When I was a child, I spake as a child, I understood as a child, I thought as a child: but when I became a man, I put away *childish things. For now we see through a glass, darkly; but then face to face: now I know in part; but then shall I know even as also I am known. And now abideth faith, hope, love, these three; but the greatest of these is love* (1 Corinthians 13).

———————

Everyone has asked himself the great question of antiquity as of the modern world: What is the *summum bonum*—the supreme good? You have life before you. Once only you can live it. What is the noblest object of desire, the supreme gift to covet?

We have been accustomed to being told that the greatest thing in the religious world is faith. That great word has been the keynote for centuries of the popular religion; and we have easily learned to look upon it as the greatest thing in the world. Well, we are wrong. If we have been told that, we may miss the mark. I have taken you, in the chapter that I have just read, to Christianity at its source; and there we have seen, "The greatest of these is love." It is not an oversight. Paul was speaking of faith just a moment before. He says, "Though I have all faith, so that I could remove mountains, and have not love, I am nothing." So, far from forgetting, he deliberately contrasts them, "Now abideth faith, hope, love," and without a moment's hesitation, the decision falls, "the greatest of these is love."

And it is not prejudice. A man is apt to recommend to others his own strong point. Love was not Paul's strong point. The observing student can detect a beautiful tenderness growing and ripening all through his character as Paul gets old; but the hand that wrote, "the greatest of these is love," when we meet it first, is stained with blood.

Nor is this letter to the Corinthians peculiar in singling out love as the *summum bonum*. The masterpieces of Christianity are agreed about it. Peter says, "Above all things have fervent love among yourselves." *Above all things.* And John goes farther, "God is love." And you remember the profound remark that Paul makes in Romans 13:10, "Love is the fulfilling of the law." Did you ever think what he meant by that? In those days men were working their passage to heaven by keeping the Ten Commandments and the hundred and ten other commandments that they had manufactured out of them. Christ said, "I will show you a more simple way. If you do one thing, you will do these hundred and ten things, without ever thinking about them. If you love, you will unconsciously fulfil the whole law." And you can readily see for yourselves how that must be so. Take any of the commandments in Deuteronomy 5. "Thou shalt have none other gods before me" (v. 7). If a man love God, you will not require to tell him that. Love is the fulfilling of that law. Take not His name in vain (v. 11). Would he ever dream of taking His name in vain if he loved Him? Remember the Sabbath day to keep it holy (v. 12). Would he not be too glad to have one day in seven to dedicate more exclusively to the object of his affection? Love would fulfill all these laws regarding God. And so, if he loved man, you would never think of telling him to honor his father and mother. He could not do anything else. It would be preposterous to tell him not to kill. You could only insult him if you suggested that he should not steal— how could he steal from those he loved? It would be superfluous to beg him not to bear false witness against his neighbor. If he loved him it would be the last thing he would do. And you would never dream of urging him not to covet what his neighbors had. He would rather they possessed it than himself. In this way "love is the fulfilling of the law." It is the rule for fulfilling all rules, the new commandment for keeping all the old commandments, Christ's one secret of the Christian life.

Now Paul had learned that; and in this noble eulogy he has given us the most wonderful and original account extant of the *summum bonum*. We may divide it into three parts. In the beginning of the short chapter, we have *love contrasted;* in the heart of it, we have *love analyzed;* toward the end we have *love defended* as the supreme gift.

The Contrast

Paul begins by contrasting love with other things that men in those days thought much of. I shall not attempt to go over those things in detail. Their inferiority is already obvious.

He contrasts it with eloquence. And what a noble gift it is, the power of playing upon the souls and wills of men, and rousing them to lofty purposes and holy deeds. Paul says, "Though I speak with the tongues of men and of angels, and have not love, I am become as sounding brass, or a tinkling cymbal." And we all know why. We have all felt the brazenness of words without emotion, the hollowness, the unaccountable unpersuasiveness of eloquence behind which lies no love.

He contrasts it with prophecy. He contrasts it with mysteries. He contrasts it with faith. He contrasts it with charity. Why is love greater than faith? Because the end is greater than the means. And why is it greater than charity? Because the whole is greater than the part. Love is greater than faith because the end is greater than the means. What is the use of having faith? It is to connect the soul with God. And what is the object of connecting man with God? That he may become like God. But God is love. Hence faith, the means, is in order to love, the end. Love, therefore, obviously is greater than faith. It is greater than charity, again, because the whole is greater than a part. Charity is only a little bit of love, one of the innumerable avenues of love, and there may even be, and there is, a great deal of charity without love. It is a very easy thing to toss a copper to a beggar in the street; it is generally an easier thing than not to do it. Yet love is just as often in the withholding. We purchase relief from the sympathetic feelings roused by the spectacle of misery, at the copper's cost. It is too cheap—too cheap for us, and often too dear for the beggar. If we really loved him we would either do more for him, or less.

Then Paul contrasts it with sacrifice and martyrdom. And I beg the little band of would-be missionaries—and I have the honor to call some of you by this name for the first time—to remember that though you give your bodies to be burned, and have not love, it profits nothing—nothing! You can take nothing greater to the heathen world than the impress and reflection of the love of God on your own character. That is the universal language. It will take you years to speak in Chinese or in the dialects of India. From the day you land, that language of love, understood by all, will be pouring forth its unconscious eloquence. It is the man who is the missionary; it is not his words. His character is his message. In the heart of Africa, among the great lakes, I have come across black men and women who remembered the only white man they ever saw before—David Livingstone; and as you cross his footsteps in that dark continent, men's faces light up as they speak of the kind doctor who passed there years ago. They could not understand him; but they felt the love that beat in his heart. Take into your new sphere of labor, where you also mean to lay down your life, that simple charm, and your life work must succeed. You can take nothing greater, you need take nothing less. It is not worthwhile going if you take anything less. You may take every accomplishment; you may be braced for every sacrifice; but if you give your body to be burned, and have not love, it will profit you and the cause of Christ *nothing*.

The Analysis

After contrasting love with these things, Paul in three verses, very short, gives us an amazing analysis of what this supreme thing is. I ask you to look at it. It is a compound thing, he tells us. It is like light. As you have seen a man of science take a beam of light and pass it through a crystal prism, as you have seen it come out on the other side of the prism broken up into its component colors—red, orange, yellow, blue, violet, and all the colors of the rainbow—so Paul passes this thing, love, through the magnificent prism of his inspired intellect, and it comes out on the other side broken up into its elements. And in these few words we have what one might call the spectrum of love, the analysis of love. Will you observe what its elements are? Will you notice that they have common names; that they are virtues that we hear about every day; that they are things that can be practised by every man in every place in life; and how, by a multitude of small things and ordinary virtues, the supreme thing, the *summum bonum,* is made up?

Patience	"Love suffereth long."
Kindness	"And is kind."
Generosity	"Love envieth not."
Humility	"Love vaunteth not itself, is not puffed up."
Courtesy	"Doth not behave itself unseemly."
Unselfishness	"Seeketh not her own."
Good Temper	"Is not easily provoked."
Guilelessness	"Thinketh no evil."
Sincerity	"Rejoiceth not in iniquity, but rejoiceth in the truth."

Patience, kindness, generosity, humility, courtesy, unselfishness, good temper, guilelessness, sincerity—these nine ingredients make up the supreme gift, the stature of the perfect man. You will observe that all are in relation to men, in relation to life, in relation to the known today and the near tomorrow, and not to the unknown eternity. We hear much of love to God; Christ spoke much of love to man. We make a great deal of peace with heaven; Christ made much of peace on earth. Religion is not a strange or added thing but the inspiration of the secular life, the breathing of an eternal spirit through this temporal world. The supreme thing, in short, is not a thing at all, but the giving of a further finish to the multitudinous words and acts that make up the sum of every common day.

There is no time to do more than make a passing note upon

each of these ingredients. Love is *patience*. This is the normal attitude of love; love passive, love waiting to begin; not in a hurry; calm; ready to do its work when the summons comes, but meantime wearing the ornament of a meek and quiet spirit. Love suffers long; beareth all things; believeth all things; hopeth all things. For love understands and therefore waits.

Kindness. Love is active. Have you ever noticed how much of Christ's life was spent in doing kind things—in *merely* doing kind things? Run over it with that in view, and you will find that He spent a great proportion of His time simply in making people happy, in doing good turns to people. There is only one thing greater than happiness in the world, and that is holiness; and it is not in our keeping; but what God *has* put in our power is the happiness of those about us, and that is largely to be secured by our being kind to them.

"The greatest thing," says someone, "a man can do for his Heavenly Father is to be kind to some of His other children." I wonder why it is that we are not all kinder than we are. How much the world needs it. How easily it is done. How instantaneously it acts. How infallibly it is remembered. How superabundantly it pays itself back—for there is no debtor in the world so honorable, so superbly honorable, as love. "Love never faileth." Love is success, love is happiness, love is life. "Love," I say, with Browning, "is energy of life."

> For life, with all it yields of joy and woe
> And hope and fear,
> Is just our chance o' the prize of learning love—
> How love might be, hath been indeed, and is.

Where love is, God is. He that dwelleth in love dwelleth in God. God is love. Therefore *love*. Without distinction, without calculation, without procrastination, love. Lavish it on the poor, where it is very easy; especially on the rich, who often need it most; most of all on our equals, where it is very difficult, and for whom perhaps we each do least of all. There is a difference between *trying to please* and *giving pleasure*. Give pleasure. Lose no chance of giving pleasure. For that is the ceaseless and anonymous triumph of a truly loving spirit. "I will pass through this world but once. Any good thing therefore that I can do, or any kindness that I can show to any human being, let me do it now. Let me not defer it or neglect it, for I shall not pass this way again."

Generosity. "Love envieth not." This is love in competition with others. Whenever you attempt a good work you will find other men doing the same kind of work, and probably doing it better. Envy them not. Envy is a feeling of ill will to those who are in the same line as ourselves, a spirit of covetousness and detraction. How little Christian work even is a protection against un-Christian feeling. That most despicable of all the unworthy moods that cloud a Christian's soul assuredly waits for us on the threshold of every work, unless we are fortified with this grace of magnanimity. Only one thing truly need the Christian envy—the large, rich, generous soul that "envieth not."

And then, after having learned all that, you leave to learn this further thing, *humility*—to put a seal on your lips and forget what you have done. After you have been kind, after Love has stolen forth into the world and done its beautiful work, go back into the shade again and say nothing about it. Love hides even from itself. Love waives even self-satisfaction. "Love vaunteth not itself, is not puffed up."

The fifth ingredient is a somewhat strange one to find in this *summum bonum: courtesy*. This is love in society, love in relation to etiquette. "Love doth not behave itself unseemly." Politeness has been defined as love in trifles. Courtesy is said to be love in little things. And the one secret of politeness is to love. Love cannot behave itself unseemly. You can put the most untutored person into the highest society, and if they have a reservoir of love in their heart, they will not behave themselves unseemly. They simply cannot do it. Carlyle said of Robert Burns that there was no truer gentleman in Europe than the plowman-poet. It was because he loved everything—the mouse, and the daisy, and all the things, great and small, that God had made. So with this simple passport he could mingle with any society, and enter courts and palaces from his little cottage on the banks of the Ayr. You know the meaning of the word *gentleman*. It means a gentle man—a man who does things gently, with love. And that is the whole art and mystery of it. The gentle man cannot in the nature of things do an ungentle, an ungentlemanly thing. The ungentle soul, the inconsiderate, unsympathetic nature cannot do anything else. "Love doth not behave itself unseemly."

Unselfishness. "Love seeketh not her own." Observe: Love seeketh not even that which is her own. In Britain the Englishman is devoted, and rightly, to his rights. But there come times when a man may exercise even the higher right of giving up his rights. Yet Paul does not summon us to give up our rights. Love strikes much deeper. It would have us not seek them at all, ignore them, eliminate the personal element altogether from our calculations. It is not hard to give up our rights. They are often external. The difficult thing is to give up ourselves. The more difficult thing still is not to seek things for ourselves at all. After we have sought them, bought them, won them, deserved them, we don't desire them anymore. Little cross then, perhaps, to give them up. But not to seek them, to look every man not on his own things but on the things of others—*id opus est*. "Seekest thou great things for thyself?" said the prophet; "*seek them not*." Why? Because there is no greatness in *things*. Things cannot be great. The only greatness is unselfish love. Even self-denial in itself is nothing, is almost a mistake. Only a great purpose or a mightier love can justify the waste. It is more difficult, I have said, not to seek our own at all than having sought it to give it up. I must take that back. It is only true of a partly selfish heart. Nothing is a hardship to love, and nothing is hard. I believe that Christ's yoke is easy. Christ's yoke is just His way of taking life. And I believe it is an easier way than any other. I believe it is a happier way than any other. The most obvious lesson in Christ's teaching is that there is no happiness in having and getting anything but only in giving. I repeat: *There is no happiness in having or in getting but only in giving.* And half the world is on the wrong scent in the pursuit of happiness. They think it consists of having and getting and in being served by others. It consists of giving and serving others. He that would be great among you, said Christ, let him serve. He that would be happy, let him remember that there is but one way—it is more blessed, it is more happy—to give than to receive.

The next ingredient is a very remarkable one: *good temper.* "Love is not easily provoked." Nothing could be more striking than to find this here. We are inclined to look on bad temper as a very harmless weakness. We speak of it as a mere infirmity of nature, a family failing, a matter of temperament, not a thing to take into very serious account in estimating a man's character. And yet here, right in the heart of this analysis of love, it finds a place; and the Bible again and again returns to condemn it as one of the most destructive elements in human nature.

The peculiarity of ill temper is that it is the vice of the virtuous. It is often the one blot on an otherwise noble character. You know men who are all but perfect and women who would be entirely perfect but for an easily ruffled, quick-tempered, or "touchy" disposition. This compatibility of ill temper with high moral character is one of the strangest and saddest problems of ethics. The truth is there are two great classes of sins—sins of the body and sins of the disposition. The Prodigal Son may be taken as a type of the first, the elder brother of the second. Now society has no doubt whatever as to which of these is the worse. Its brands falls, without a challenge, on the Prodigal. But are we right? We have no balance to weigh one another's sins, and coarser and finer are but human words; but faults in the higher nature may be less venial than those in the lower, and to the eye of Him who is love, a sin against love may seem a hundred times more base. No form of vice, not worldliness, not greed of gold, not drunkenness itself, does more to un-Christianize society than evil temper. For embittering life, for breaking up communities, for destroying the most sacred relationships, for devastating homes, for withering up men and women, for taking the bloom off childhood; in short, for sheer gratuitous misery-producing power, this influence stands alone. Look at the elder brother, moral, hard-working, patient, dutiful—let him get all credit for his virtues—look at this man, this baby, sulking outside his own father's door. "He was angry," we read, "and would not go in." Look at the effect on the father, on the servants, on the happiness of the guests. Judge of the effect upon the Prodigal—and how many prodigals are kept out of the kingdom of God by the unlovely characters of those who profess to be inside? Analyze, as a study in temper, the thundercloud itself as it gathers on the elder brother's brow. What is it made of? Jealousy, anger, pride, uncharity, cruelty, self-righteousness, touchiness, doggedness, sullenness—these are the ingredients of this dark and loveless soul. In varying proportions, also, these are the ingredients of all ill temper. Judge if such sins of the disposition are not worse to live in, and for others to live with, than sins of the body. Did Christ indeed not answer the question Himself when He said, "I say unto you, that the publicans and the harlots go into the kingdom of heaven before you." There is really no place in heaven for a disposition like this. A man with such a mood could only make heaven miserable for all the people in it. Except, therefore, such a man be born again, he cannot, he simply *cannot,* enter the kingdom of heaven. For it is perfectly certain—and you will not misunderstand me—that to enter heaven a man must take it with him.

You will see then why temper is significant. It is not in what it is alone but in what it reveals. This is why I take the liberty now of speaking of it with such unusual plainness. It is a test for love, a symptom, a revelation of an unloving nature at bottom. It is the intermittent fever that bespeaks unintermittent disease within; the occasional bubble escaping to the surface that betrays some rottenness underneath; a sample of the most hidden products of the soul dropped involuntarily when off one's guard; in a word, the lightning form of a hundred hideous and un-Christian sins. For a want of patience, a want of kindness, a want of generosity, a want of courtesy, a want of unselfishness, are all instantaneously symbolized in one flash of temper.

Hence it is not enough to deal with the temper. We must go to the source and change the inmost nature, and the angry humors will die away of themselves. Souls are made sweet not by taking the acid fluids out but by putting something in—a great love, a new spirit, the spirit of Christ. Christ, the spirit of Christ, interpenetrating ours, sweetens, purifies, transforms all. This only can eradicate what is wrong, work a chemical change, renovate and regenerate, and rehabilitate the inner man. Will power does not change men. Time does not change men. Christ does. Therefore, "Let that mind be in you which was also in Christ Jesus." Some of us have not much time to lose. Remember, once more, that this is a matter of life or death. I cannot help speaking urgently, for myself, for yourselves. "Whoso shall offend one of these little ones, which believe in me, it were better for him that a millstone were hanged about his neck, and that he were drowned in the depth of the sea." That is to say, it is the deliberate verdict of the Lord Jesus that it is better not to live than not to love. *It is better not to live than not to love.*

Guilelessness and sincerity may be dismissed almost with a word. Guilelessness is having the grace for suspicious people. And the possession of it is the great secret of personal influence.

You will find, if you think for a moment, that the people who influence you are people who believe in you. In an atmosphere of suspicion men shrivel up; but in that atmosphere they expand and find encouragement and educative fellowship. It is a wonderful thing that here and there in this hard, uncharitable world there should still be left a few rare souls who think no evil. This is the great unworldliness. Love "thinketh no evil," imputes no motive, sees the bright side, puts the best construction on every action. What a delightful state of mind to live in! What a stimulus and benediction even to meet with it for a day! To be trusted is to be saved. And if we try to influence or elevate others, we shall soon see that success is in proportion to their belief of our belief in them. For the respect of another is the first restoration of the self-respect a man has lost; our ideal of what he is becomes to him the hope and pattern of what he may become.

"Love rejoiceth not in iniquity, but rejoiceth in the truth." I have called this *sincerity* from the words rendered in the Authorized Version by "rejoiceth in the truth." And, certainly, were this the real translation, nothing could be more just. For he who loves will love truth not less than men. He will rejoice in the truth—rejoice not in what he has been taught to believe; not in this church's doctrine or in that; not in this ism or in that ism; but "in the truth." He will accept only what is real; he will strive to get at facts; he will search for truth with a humble and unbiased mind, and cherish whatever he finds at any sacrifice. But the more literal translation of the Revised Version calls for just such a sacrifice for truth's sake here. For what Paul really meant is, as we there read, "Rejoiceth not in unrighteousness, but rejoiceth with the truth," a quality that probably no one English word—and certainly not *sincerity*—adequately defines. It includes, perhaps more strictly, the self-restraint that refuses to make capital out of others' faults; the charity that delights not in exposing the weakness of others but "covereth all things;" the sincerity of purpose that endeavors to see things as they are and rejoices to find them better than suspicion feared or calumny denounced.

So much for the analysis of love. Now the business of our lives is to have these things fitted into our characters. That is the supreme work to which we need to address ourselves in this world—to learn love. Is life not full of opportunities for learning love? Every man and woman everyday has a thousand of them. The world is not a playground; it is a schoolroom. Life is not a holiday but an education. And the one eternal lesson for us all is: *how better we can love.* What makes a man a good cricketer? Practice. What makes a man a good artist, a good sculptor, a good musician? Practice. What makes a man a good linguist, a good stenographer? Practice. What makes a man a good man? Practice. Nothing else. There is nothing capricious about religion. We do not get the soul in different ways, under different laws, from those in which we get the body and the mind. If a man does not exercise his arm, he develops no biceps muscle; and if a man does not exercise his soul, he acquires no muscle in his soul, no strength of character, no vigor of moral fiber, no beauty of spiritual growth. Love is not a thing of enthusiastic emotion. It is a rich, strong, manly, vigorous expression of the whole round Christian character—the Christlike nature in its fullest development. And the constituents of this great character are only to be built up by ceaseless practice.

What was Christ doing in the carpenter's shop? Practicing. Though perfect, we read that He learned obedience, He *increased* in wisdom and in favor with God and man. Do not quarrel therefore with your lot in life. Do not complain of its never-ceasing cares, its petty environment, the vexations you have to stand, the small and sordid souls you have to live and work with. Above all, do not resent temptation; do not be perplexed because it seems to thicken round you more and more and ceases neither for effort nor for agony nor prayer. That is the practice that God appoints you; and it is having its work in making you patient, humble, generous, unselfish, kind, and courteous. Do not grudge the hand that is molding the still too shapeless image within you. It is growing more beautiful though you see it not, and every touch of temptation may add to its perfection. Therefore keep in the midst of life. Do not isolate yourself. Be among men, and among things, and among troubles, and difficulties, and obstacles. You remember Goethe's words: *Es bildet ein Talent sich in der Stille, Doch ein Character in dem Strom der Welt.* "Talent develops itself in solitude; character in the stream of life." Talent develops itself in solitude—the talent of prayer, of faith, of meditation, of seeing the unseen; character grows in the stream of the world's life. That chiefly is where men are to learn love.

How? To make it easier, I have named a few of the elements of love. But these are only elements. Love itself can never be defined. Light is a something more than the sum of its ingredients—a glowing, dazzling, tremulous ether. And love is something more than all its elements—a palpitating, quivering, sensitive, living thing. By synthesis of all the colors, men can make whiteness; they cannot make light. By synthesis of all the virtues, men can make virtue; they cannot make love. How then are we to have this transcendent living whole conveyed into our souls? We brace our wills to secure it. We try to copy those who have it. We lay down rules about it. We watch. We pray. But these things alone will not bring love into our natures. Love is an *effect.* And only as we fulfil the right condition can we have the effect produced. Shall I tell you what the *cause* is?

If you turn to the Revised Version of the First Epistle of John you will find these words: "We love, because He first loved us." "We love," not "We love *Him.*" That is the way the old version has it, and it is quite wrong. "*We love*—because He first loved us." Look at that word *because.* It is the *cause* of which I have spoken. "*Because* He first loved us," the effect follows that we love; we love Him; we love all men. We cannot help it. Because He loved us, we love, we love everybody. Our hearts are slowly changed. Contemplate the love of Christ, and you will love. Stand before that mirror, reflect Christ's character, and you will be changed into the same image from tenderness to tenderness. There is no other way. You cannot love to order. You can only look at the lovely object, and fall in love with it, and grow into likeness to it. And so look at this perfect character, this perfect life. Look at the great sacrifice as He laid down Himself, all through life, and upon the cross of Calvary; and you must love Him. And loving Him, you must become like Him. Love begets love. It is a process of induction. Put a piece of iron in the presence of a magnetized body and that piece of iron for a time becomes magnetized. It is charged with an attractive force in the mere presence of the original force, and as long as you leave the two side by side, they are both magnets alike. Remain side by side with Him who loved us and gave Himself for us, and you too will become a center of power, a permanently attractive force; and like Him you will draw all men unto you, like Him you will be drawn unto all men. That is the inevitable effect of love. Any man who fulfils that cause must have that effect produced in him. Try to give up the idea that religion comes to us by chance, or by mystery, or by caprice. It comes to us by natural law, or by supernatural law, for all law is divine. Edward Irving went to see a dying boy once, and when he entered the room he just put his hand on the sufferer's head and said, "My boy, God loves you," and went away. And the boy started from his bed, and called out to the people in the house, "God loves me! God loves me!" It changed that boy. The sense that God loved him overpowered him, melted him down, and began the creating of a new heart in him. And that is how the love of God melts down the unlovely heart in humans and begets in them the new creature, who is patient and humble and gentle and unselfish.

And there is no other way to get it. There is no mystery about it. We love others, we love everybody, we love our enemies because He first loved us.

The Defense

Now I have a closing sentence or two to add about Paul's reason for singling out love as the supreme possession. It is a very remarkable reason. In a single sentence it is this: It lasts. "Love," urges Paul, "never faileth." Then he begins again one of his marvellous lists of the great things of the day and exposes them one by one. He runs over the things that men thought were going to last and shows that they are all fleeting, temporary, passing away.

"Whether there be prophecies, they shall fail." It was a mother's ambition for her boy in those days that he should become a prophet. For hundreds of years God had never spoken by means of any prophet, and at that time the prophet was greater than the king. Men waited wistfully for another messenger to come, and hung on his every word when he appeared as on the very voice of God. Paul says, "Whether there be prophecies, they shall fail." This Book is full of prophecies. One by one they have "failed"; that is, having been fulfilled their work is finished; they have nothing more to do now in the world except to feed a devout man's faith.

Then Paul talks about tongues. That was another thing that was greatly coveted. "Whether there be tongues, they shall cease." As we all know, many centuries have passed since tongues have been known in this world. They have ceased. Take it in any sense you like. Take it, for illustration merely, as languages in general—a sense that was not in Paul's mind at all, and that though it cannot give us the specific lesson will point the general truth. Consider the words in which these chapters were written—Greek. It has gone. Take the Latin—the other great tongue of those days. It ceased long ago. Look at the Indian language. It is ceasing. The language of Wales, of Ireland, of the Scottish Highlands is dying before our eyes. The most popular book in the English tongue at the present time, except the Bible, is one of Dickens's works, his *Pickwick Papers*. It is largely written in the language of London street life; and experts assure us that in fifty years it will be unintelligible to the average English reader.

Then Paul goes farther, and with even greater boldness adds, "Whether there be knowledge, it shall vanish away." The wisdom of the ancients, where is it? It is wholly gone. A schoolboy today knows more than Sir Isaac Newton knew. His knowledge has vanished away. You put yesterday's paper in the fire. Its knowledge has vanished away. You buy the old editions of the great encyclopedias for a few pence. Their knowledge has vanished away. Look how the coach has been superseded by the use of steam. Look how electricity has superseded that and swept a hundred almost new inventions into oblivion. One of the greatest living authorities, Sir William Thomson, said the other day, "The steam-engine is passing away." "Whether there be knowledge, it shall vanish away." At every workshop you will see, in the backyard, a heap of old iron, a few wheels, a few levers, a few cranks, broken and eaten with rust. Twenty years ago that was the pride of the city. Men flocked in from the country to see the great invention; now it is superseded, its day is done. And all the boasted science and philosophy of this day will soon be old. But yesterday in the University of Edinburgh, the greatest figure in the faculty was Sir James Simpson, the discoverer of chloroform. The other day his successor and nephew, Professor Simpson, was asked by the librarian of the university to go to the library and pick out the books on his subject that were no longer needed. And his reply to the librarian was this: "Take every text book that is more than ten years old, and put it down in the cellar." Sir James Simpson was a great authority only a few years ago: men came from all parts of the earth to consult him; and almost the whole teaching of that time is consigned by the science of today to oblivion. And in every branch of science it is the same. "Now we know in part. We see through a glass darkly."

Can you tell me anything that is going to last? Many things Paul did not condescend to name. He did not mention money, fortune, fame; but he picked out the great things of his time, the things that the best men thought had something in them, and brushed them peremptorily aside. Paul had no charge against these things in themselves. All he said about them was that they would not last. They were great things, but not supreme things. There were things beyond them. What we are stretches past what we do, beyond what we possess. Many things that men denounce as sins are not sins; but they are temporary. And that is a favorite argument of the New Testament. John says of the world, not that it is wrong, but simply that it "passeth away." There is a great deal in the world that is delightful and beautiful; there is a great deal in it that is great and engrossing; but it will not last. All that is in the world, the lust of the eye, the lust of the flesh, and the pride of life, are but for a little while. Love not the world therefore. Nothing that it contains is worth the life and consecration of an immortal soul. The immortal soul must give itself to something that is immortal. And the only immortal things are these: "Now abideth faith, hope, love, but the greatest of these is love."

Some think that the time will come when two of these three things will also pass away—faith into sight, hope into fruition. Paul does not say so. We know but little now about the conditions of the life that is to come. But what is certain is that love must last. God, the eternal God, is Love. Covet therefore that everlasting gift, that one thing that it is certain is going to stand, that one coinage that will be current in the universe when all the other coinages of all the nations of the world shall be useless and unhonored. You will give yourselves to many things, give yourselves first to love. Hold things in their proportion. *Hold things in their proportion.* Let at least the first great object of our lives be to achieve the character defended in these words, the character—and it is the character of Christ—that is built around love.

I have said that this thing is eternal. Did you ever notice how continually John associates love and faith with eternal life? I was not told when I was a boy that "God so loved the world that He gave His only begotten Son, that whosoever believeth in Him should not perish, but have everlasting life." What I was told, I remember, was that God so loved the world that, if I trusted in Him, I was to have a thing called peace, or I was to have rest, or I was to have joy, or I was to have safety. But I had to find out for myself that whosoever trusteth in Him—that is, whosoever loveth Him, for trust is only the avenue to love—hath everlasting life. The gospel offers a man life. Never offer men a thimbleful of gospel. Do not offer them merely joy, or merely peace, or merely rest, or merely safety; tell them how Christ came to give men a more abundant life than they have, a life abundant in love, and therefore abundant in salvation for themselves, and large in enterprise for the alleviation and redemption of the world. Then only can the gospel take hold of the whole of a man, body, soul, and spirit, and give to each part of his nature its exercise and reward. Many of the current gospels are addressed only to a part of man's nature. They offer peace, not life; faith, not love; justification, not regeneration. And men slip back again from such religion because it has never really held them. Their nature was not all in it. It offered no deeper and gladder life-current than the life that was lived before. Surely it stands to reason that only a fuller love can compete with the love of the world.

To love abundantly is to live abundantly, and to love forever is to live forever. Hence, eternal life is inextricably bound up with love. We want to live forever for the same reason that we want to live tomorrow. Why do you want to live tomorrow? It is because there is someone who loves you, and whom you want to see tomorrow, and be with, and love back. There is no other reason why we should live on than that we love and are beloved. It is when a man has no one to love him that he commits suicide. So long as he has friends, those who love him and whom he loves, he will live; because to live is to love. Be it but the love of a dog, it will keep him in life; but let that go, and he has no contact with life, no reason to live. The "energy of life" has failed. Eternal life also is to know God, and God is Love. This is Christ's own definition. Ponder it. "This is life eternal, that they might know Thee the only true God, and Jesus Christ whom Thou hast sent." Love must be eternal. It is what God is. On the last analysis, then, love is life. Love never faileth, and life never faileth, so long as there is love. That is the philosophy of what Paul is showing us; the reason why in the nature of things love should be the supreme thing—because it is going to last; because in the nature of things, it is an eternal life. That life is a thing that we are living now, not that we get when we die; that we shall have a poor chance of getting when we die unless we are living now. No worse fate can befall a man in this world than to live and grow old alone, unloving and unloved. To be lost is to live in an unregenerate condition, loveless and unloved; and to be saved is to love; and he that dwelleth in love dwelleth already in God. For God is love.

Now I have all but finished. How many of you will join me in reading this chapter once a week for the next three months? A man did that once and it changed his whole life. Will you do it? It is for the greatest thing in the world. You might begin by reading it every day, especially the verses which describe the perfect character. "Love suffereth long, and is kind; love envieth not; love vaunteth not itself." Get these ingredients into your life. Then everything that you do is eternal. It is worth doing. It is worth giving time to. No man can become a saint in his sleep; and to fulfill the condition required demands a certain amount of prayer and meditation and time, just as improvement in any direction, bodily or mental, requires preparation and care. Address yourself to that one thing; at any cost have this transcendent character exchanged for yours. You will find as you look back on your life that the moments that stand out, the moments when you have really lived, are the moments when you have done things in a spirit of love. As memory scans the past, above and beyond all the transitory pleasures of life, there leap forward those supreme hours when you have been enabled to do unnoticed kindnesses to those around about you, things too trifling to speak about, but that you feel have entered into your eternal life. I have seen almost all the beautiful things that God has made; I have enjoyed almost every pleasure that He has planned for man; and yet as I look back, I see standing out above all the life that has gone four or five short experiences when the love of God reflected itself in some poor imitation, some small act of love of mine, and these seem to be the things that alone of all one's life abide. Everything else in all our lives is transitory. Every other good is visionary. But the acts of love that no man knows about or can ever know about—they never fail.

In the book of Matthew, where the Judgment Day is depicted for us in the imagery of One seated on a throne and dividing the sheep from the goats, the test of a man then is not, "How have I believed?" but "How have I loved?" The test of religion, the final test of religion, is not religiousness, but love. I say the final test of religion at that great day is not religiousness, but love; not what I have done, not what I have believed, not what I have achieved, but how I have discharged the common charities of life. Sins of commission in that awful indictment are not even referred to. By what we have not done, *by sins of omission,* we are judged. It could not be otherwise. For the withholding of love is the negation of the spirit of Christ, the proof that we never knew Him, that for us He lived in vain. It means that He suggested nothing in all our thoughts, that He inspired nothing in all our lives, that we were not once near enough to Him to be seized with the spell of His compassion for the world. It means that:

> I lived for myself, I thought for myself,
> For myself, and none beside—
> Just as if Jesus had never lived,
> As if He had never died.

It is the Son of Man before whom the nations of the world shall be gathered. It is in the presence of *humanity* that we shall be charged. And the spectacle itself, the mere sight of it, will silently judge each one. Those will be there whom we have met and helped; or there, the unpitied multitude whom we neglected or despised. No other witness need be summoned. No other charge than lovelessness shall be preferred. Be not deceived. The words that all of us shall one day hear, sound not of theology but of life, not of churches and saints but of the hungry and the poor, not of creeds and doctrines but of shelter and clothing, not of Bibles and prayer books but of cups of cold water in the name of Christ. Thank God the Christianity of today is coming nearer the world's need. Live to help that on. Thank God men know better, by a hairbreadth, what religion is, what God is, who Christ is, where Christ is. Who is Christ? He who fed the hungry, clothed the naked, visited the sick. And where is Christ? Where?—whoso shall receive a little child in My name receiveth Me. And who are Christ's? Everyone that loveth is born of God.

| 2 |

The Three Faces of Love

See how great a love the Father has bestowed upon us.

1 John 3:1

Love! What a pungent, intriguing word! Love stimulates our imaginations, conjures up dreams, creates fantasies, carries us away on the wings of sheer joy. The movies, television, novels, the Internet, and a million other media saturate us with the idea. Even the Bible speaks of it untold times, actually telling us that God is Love. What can it all mean? Henry Drummond certainly captured it; he called love the greatest thing in the world. If he can be trusted to be right—and surely he can—we need to find out about that word. But to uncover the untold riches of the term, we shall be compelled to put our hands to the plowshares and cut deep furrows in the field of inquiry. Yet it will have its reward, for if all that Drummond has said about love is true, it can lead to the discovery of what life is all about. The plowing required may at times seem more like plodding. But it will have its compensation; a properly cultivated field can yield an abundant crop. So we sink the blade deep into the rich soil of truth and begin to turn over the sod.

One cannot read—or reread—Henry Drummond's classic presentation of 1 Corinthians 13 without drawing the same conclusion as did the author; the greatest thing in the world truly is *love*. As he put it, love becomes the *summum bonum* of life. Drummond clearly pointed out that this basic fact finds its foundation in the truth of Scripture, everyday experiences of life, the logic inherent in the idea, and above all, the revelation of the very nature of God Himself. Love rightly ascends to a central role in all of life. Thus, it will be well worth delving into the theme with enthusiasm to uncover an in-depth grasp of the experience, for love is intended to be experienced as well as truth to be understood.

In everyday language, the word *love* bristles with a multitude of meanings, some considerably contrasting the other. To say one loves his or her neighbor presents a quite different interpretation of the term than to say that one loves chocolate ice cream. It is radically different from saying one loves God with all of the heart, soul, strength, and mind. Yet in the English language we find ourselves shackled to the use of one simple little word. Unfortunately, love has to be employed to cover a broad spectrum of ideas. Thus, we face a rather difficult situation at times to express how we genuinely feel.

Fortunately, such is not the case in the beautiful language in which the New Testament unfolds. The writers of the New Testament penned their works in the expressive Greek language; a tongue universally understood throughout the Mediterranean world in the first century. God in His providence guided the development of the language into a wonderfully diverse and descriptive medium for conveying His eternal truth. Greek became a picturesque, pungent, and very penetrating medium. And when the various shades of the concept of love are demanded, the Greek language rises to the occasion. Different, at times quite radically different, connotations for the one English word *love* can be found in at least three distinct Greek terms. Those primary words for love in the expressive language of the New Testament era are *eros, philia,* and *agape*.

A rapid run through the Scriptures—which we shall undertake in this chapter—will bring out something of the power of these three different terms and how they relate to a Christian seeking to love as God requires. No attempt will be made to be laborious or technical. We shall try to follow Henry Drummond's philosophy of expressing profound biblical truths simply. But we should also realize, as C. S. Lewis put it so well, "It's no good asking for a simple religion. After all, real things are not simple."[1] So we will run the risk of not sounding too simple so as to miss the point. Coming to an understanding of these pungent Greek words assumes significant importance if we wish to grasp in some depth what Henry Drummond attempted to communicate and see what the Bible itself means when it tells us to love.

It should be understood at the outset that some of the Greek words we will center on are used in the Bible interchangeably at times (for example John 12:43). But for the better part, the New Testament maintains a quite clear distinction among the various terms, as shall become evident. These distinctions will help the love theme grip our minds forcibly and clearly. So we launch out, hoping to arrive at what the Word of God means by love and how the different terms relate to the passages of Scripture that will unfold. Therefore, we travel back into the first century to see just what the inspired writers of the New Testament were talking about when they chose one of the three basic words at their disposal—*eros, philia,* and *agape.* We begin our pilgrimage with *eros.*

Eros

It may appear rather strange to begin the quest for Christian love by looking at a word that does not actually appear in the Bible. The Greek word *eros,* normally translated "love," cannot be found even once in the Holy Scriptures. Then why labor the point? For several reasons; first, eros stands in such stark contradiction to God's standard and meaning of love that it becomes very important to grasp the general motif of an eros kind of love. A study of eros will make the true love of God stand out in bold relief. And even if the word itself does not occur in the New Testament, the idea behind the term surely does; and the Scriptures stand unequivocally opposed to this level of love.

Moreover, a quick glance at the world makes it abundantly clear that eros love crowds in all about us; it dominates lost people whom God sent His Son to save. Unless God's quality of love becomes the essential motif of life through Jesus Christ, eros remains the only primary alternative. And that is serious indeed because eros is eternally ruining.

Platonic Love

Eros love covers a broad spectrum of meaning, all the way from crude, fleshly eroticism to a considerably higher level of understanding. The highest concept of love from the eros perspective emerged in the thought of Plato, the great Greek philosopher. Plato is not the easiest thinker to understand; nonetheless, we will do well to delve for a moment into his basic approach and see what he thinks of love because much of the world's grasp of life and love centers in his thought.

To get at what Plato meant by *eros,* we must first realize that in his view of love (he almost always used the term *eros* in his writings), the idea of sordid, sensual eroticism is all but absent. The famous philosopher had a far more "spiritual" approach. He assumed, as did many in his day, that the human soul has a supernatural, divine origin. Hence, it possesses great worth; actually it possesses immortality. Not only that, Plato argued that the immortal human soul lived in or experienced a preexistent state with the gods, and furthermore, he held to the view of reincarnation. The philosopher believed in the panoply of the Greek gods, not in the one and only true God of the Bible. But as he saw it, because the human soul once dwelt with these gods before life on earth, it got filled with a heavenly vision. All people still retain a vague memory of the glory of the flawless world of the heavenlies and feel a strange, compelling drawing to that ideal, heavenly world. That longing for the divine presence is described by the word *eros*. As one author put it:

Just as the stone in virtue of its nature is attracted downwards, so the soul in virtue of its divine nature is attracted upwards; for everything in existence strives to find its own natural place. *This upward attraction of the soul is Eros*. It is something in the world of souls analogous to the law of gravitation in the natural world. It prevents the soul from settling down in things temporal, and reminds it that here it is but a stranger and a sojourner.[2]

Simply put, love in Plato's teaching centers in the heavenly eros—a love striving for the bright, beautiful world of eternity where the gods dwell. It can be expressed as a deep longing to participate in the divine life itself. That approach to love obviously constitutes a far cry from the eroticism of the flesh, although Plato employs the same Greek word.

For Plato, "*eros* is love for the beautiful and the good,"[3] as it leads ultimately to the divine level, even if it may get somewhat perverted on the way. Or to express it in another manner, eros becomes the way to heaven. Striving for heaven may appear reasonable and even good on the surface, but it is a far cry from what the Bible means by love or as a way to God.

Anders Nygren in his classic volume, *Agape and Eros*, tells us that three primary ideas emerge out of the Platonic concept of love: "(1) Eros is the 'love of desire,' or acquisitive love; (2) Eros is man's way to the Divine; (3) Eros is egocentric love."[4] And here is where the eros perversion of God's quality of love can be clearly visualized and where so many have been deceived.

Acquisitive Eros Love. Eros as acquisitive love manifests itself as a desire, a longing, a striving for what we do not have. As a consequence, love in this eros sense has two primary characteristics: a consciousness of need and an effort to find satisfaction in fulfilling that need. Quite clearly, this means that eros love becomes the motivation to acquire some object or goal that it regards as beautiful and valuable in making one happy. Love, in this Platonic sense, is thus a motivated love, an acquisitive love, a seeking after value and satisfaction. Personal happiness becomes the primary goal. We see this manifestation of eros throughout the entire world. The quest for that higher and happier state consumes multitudes continually. It can even express itself as crass materialism or the striving for fame or popularity. Satisfaction of life is all that really counts.

Eros: The Way to the Divine. Plato, as pointed out, held to the typical religious concepts of his day. He believed in many gods. Eros, the striving for the highest good, thus becomes the way into fellowship with these gods. A relationship with the gods is the highest, happiest state, at least as Plato saw it. This, therefore, becomes the religious expression of eros love. Consequently, Plato argued that eros stands as the mediator between the gods and human life. Eros lifts people up in their imperfection to the perfection of deity, the mortal to immortality. Little wonder, therefore, that Plato speaks of love as the seeking of the divine life. People love in the eros sense because they want to get to where the happy gods are and thus be completely satisfied. Many get sidetracked on the way by materialism, sensuality, or whatever. Still, heaven is subconsciously the end of their striving. Therefore, simply put, eros becomes the means by which any person can scale the mountain peak of the divine and finally arrive in its presence. That point becomes vitally important for Christians to grasp.

This now leads to the third and final aspect of Plato's understanding of eros. And the crunch for Christian believers in Jesus Christ surfaces clearly.

Egocentric Eros Love. We can correctly conclude that the entire philosophical structure of Plato's understanding of love is essentially egocentric, that is, utterly human centered.

Everything, absolutely everything, revolves around the individual self and its self-centered quest for the highest happiness. From first to last, the soul that is seeking immortality is aflame with egocentric striving, that is, with eros. True, eros love operates in bondage to the body (which all the Greeks saw as sinful flesh), but it gradually rises above the body, enabling one to ascend to the level of the eternal world with its blessed vision of glory in the presence of the gods.

The very fact that eros is an acquisitive, motivated kind of love demonstrates its self-seeking nature. All desire and longing is more or less egocentric. Little wonder, therefore, that Plato said, "It is by the acquisition of good things, that the happy are made happy."[5] Thus, it follows that since all people want to be happy, all people love and strive for the good. And what is that ultimate good? Immortality with the gods! Eros, therefore, must always be understood as the pathway to immortality.

As these doctrines of Plato developed through subsequent thinkers, some five hundred years later in what came to be known as Neoplatonism, the whole eros concept took on a religious, cultic flavor. One can even begin to see this emerging near the end of the first century. Some say that the early inklings of this Neoplatonic approach to truth came under fire by John in his first epistle when he insisted that Jesus Christ came in the flesh and that to deny such a basic truth was to deny the heart of God's revelation. Plato, and especially the Neoplatonists, could not conceive of God's actually coming down to earth in flesh as a man and touching human beings because of His love for them; thus procuring salvation. No god could ever be robed in corrupt human flesh in their thinking. The Platonic quest centered in escaping the limitations of the flesh. They saw the material aspects of reality as essentially evil. And the gods do not love people anyway, let alone come to us in a material manner for our eternal good. But the incarnation of the Son of God for our salvation lies at the very core of the Christian faith. Therefore, eros love becomes a complete perversion of basic Christianity. That explains John's attack on the Greek thought system.

As the Greeks believed that nothing good could dwell in the flesh, human ethical responsibility thus centers in rejecting this world and climbing and scaling the heights into the presence of God by one's own efforts to escape the imprisonment of the body. People must *work* for their fellowship with God. They must exercise eros. That lies at the center of their basic understanding of love. They know nothing of grace. For the Greeks, it was all egocentric, humanistic striving. Therefore, the whole Christian faith falls apart if one embraces such erroneous ideas. And a mere glance at the world today makes it clear that multitudes of people have given themselves to the error of eros in striving to find God and happiness.

Such made up the cultural mind-set that Paul had to deal with when he went to the Gentile world to preach Christ and the *true* love of God. How difficult it must have been for the apostle because the essence of the gospel revolves around the fact that God, in *His* gracious love (the opposite of eros), reaches down in Jesus Christ, His incarnate Son, to poor human beings in their egocentric striving for immortality and earthly things. He snatches them in grace out of their spiritual, sinful, self-oriented, self-seeking syndrome and brings them into His fellowship by sheer grace because of His great agape love. How different that is than eros. That is probably why Paul wrote to the Colossians: "See to it that no one takes you captive through philosophy and empty deception, according to the tradition of men, according to the elementary principles of the world, rather than according to Christ" (Col. 2:8). Tragically, however, eros is where most people find themselves. And, as Henry Drummond expressed it so well, "There is no happiness in having, or in getting, but only in giving. And half the world is on the wrong scent in the pursuit of happiness"— let alone encountering God.

Little wonder, therefore, that the word *eros* is never used in the New Testament to describe true love. To the contrary, it stands absolutely opposed to anything and everything that the Christian faith declares. Eros is human striving, essentially egocentric, and it presents a seriously perverted view of how one finds the "happier state," that is, how one finds God. It leaves no place for God in love coming to people in their needs. No room is given to grace; it is all human effort. It can even degenerate into sheer eroticism. If one sees the sensual things of this world as beautiful, then the perversion becomes complete. Many of the Greek pagan temples of worship in the first century actually had cultic prostitutes. Conclusion: Eros love stands completely contrary to the gospel of Jesus Christ.

The sadness of the situation centers in the fact that the world so often fails to see all that eros implies. As a simple, somewhat parabolic case in point, in the heart of London, England, stands a statue of the Greek god Eros; or as we often call it today, Cupid. At Piccadilly Circus millions have viewed the famous landmark. Few know, however, that it was erected to commemorate the memory of Lord Shaftesbury, a great Christian philanthropist. In Victorian Britain, all the nation admired Shaftesbury's benevolent acts of love. So they raised a statue of Eros in his honor. Being a committed believer in Jesus Christ, Shaftesbury would not want his name linked with Plato's understanding of eros love. He was a devoted follower of Jesus Christ and lived his life on the level of God's quality of love. But the world usually fails to see the distinction. Multitudes seemingly cannot conceive of valuing anything that does not have its roots in egocentric effort. They fail to understand Christ's sacrifice and God's grace. As Paul said, "A natural man does not accept the things of the Spirit of God; for they are foolishness to him, and he cannot understand them, because they are spiritually appraised" (1 Cor. 2:14).

Thus, we conclude that the entire eros system stands

spiritually flawed and an utter perversion of how to experience God and His love or to achieve happiness. Plato did not give us the way to life; actually, it is the way of spiritual bondage and death. And herein lies the great deception: Eros is exactly where people find themselves *before discovering Christ*. They wrestle in its clutches. To understand this becomes essential if one is to grasp true love. Human effort does not, cannot, procure salvation and life. As Paul put it, the Law only condemns; life comes by grace alone. That is why all this deep digging through Plato's thought becomes important. Eros stands as the world's great deceiver, and we must grasp this opposite of God's love to appreciate what His great love truly means. Satan is the master of deceit; our role centers in permitting the Spirit of God in love to remove the blinders so the world can comprehend the good news of Jesus Christ.

Incidentally, there can also be found in the circle of Greek thought another sort of humanistic love that deserves brief mention in this general context. The word is *storge*. It has no religious connotation, however. It simply implies an affectionate kind of love, especially of parents to their children and of offspring to parents. C. S. Lewis says it can even be found, at least in a very limited sense, in the animal kingdom. This love arises because of familiarity and similarity between the lovers. C. S. Lewis calls it the "humblest love."[6] We really need not spend time with this word as it cannot be found in the New Testament, and it does not lead to the higher loves we must now examine, the level of love found in the Scriptures.

What then is God's love like? What does the Bible mean when it says that He is love and commands us to love the Lord our God with all of our hearts, souls, strengths, minds, and bodies; and to love our neighbors as ourselves? In seeking this vital answer to love's deepest meaning, we turn to a word for love that is used in the New Testament writings.

Philia

The second term in the Greek language normally translated "love" is the expressive word *philia*. In the secular sense, a simple definition in its verbal form connotes the idea of regarding or treating someone as one's own people. It presents the idea of a natural attraction to those who belong to our group. It was often used in the first century in everyday conversation to express love for a close relative or a spouse or child. In that sense it somewhat approximates *storge*. At times it speaks of friendship or admiration. It can even be used for the master's love for his servants. *Philia* always implies an element of preference or favor. Quite naturally, therefore, it is especially used for the love of close friends. Thus, it often reflects the idea of helping or assisting someone greatly admired.

The question now arises, How did the biblical writers understand and use this word? What makes up its spiritual meanings? First of all, it approximates on a few occasions the unique word used to describe the love of God, *agape*. We can see this usage clearly in the conversation between the Lord Jesus and Peter after the Resurrection as recorded in John 21:15-17:

> "Simon, son of John, do you love *[agape]* Me more than these?" He said to Him, "Yes, Lord; You know that I love *[philia]* You." He said to him, "Tend My lambs." He said to him again a second time, "Simon, son of John, do you love *[agape]* Me?" He said to Him, "Yes, Lord; You know that I love *[philia]* You." He said to him, "Shepherd My sheep." He said to him a third time, "Simon, son of John, do you love *[philia]* Me?" Peter was grieved because He said to him the third time, "Do you love *[philia]* Me?" And he said to Him, "Lord, You know all things; You know that I love *[philia]* You." Jesus said to him, "Tend My sheep."

The central thrust of the passage rests on Jesus' recommissioning of Peter after his threefold denial of the Lord. As one scholar put it, "The threefold questioning of the love of Peter for Jesus is certainly to be related . . . to the threefold denial of Peter . . . (and) by threefold installation in the pastoral office Jesus proclaims to him forgiveness for his betrayal."[7] In the dialogue between Jesus and Peter, it seems that the words *philia* and *agape* were used interchangeably, although some Bible scholars make a point over the use of the two different words. Further, on one or more occasions John employed *philia* to connote the Father's "intimate affection" for His children (see John 16:27). *Agape* still becomes the major term to speak of God's love. We have not yet attempted to define the rich meaning of agape, that shall come later; the important thing to see here is that philia rises far above eros in content as it relates to the Christian life.

Love on the philia, more spiritual level, gives the idea of value; to love something or someone because of the intrinsic value of love's object. It can even in certain contexts be properly translated, "to kiss." The principle of the spiritual kiss can also be found often in the Old Testament. For example, in Proverbs 24:26, we read, "He kisses the lips who gives a right answer." The kiss of love in the philia sense became firmly rooted in Jewish custom. From time to time in the Old Testament it signified proof of reconciliation (Ps. 2:12). In Genesis 48:10 it ratified an adoption, and in Genesis 27:26-30 it was given as a blessing. Quite naturally, the kiss of love was rejected when it slipped into the more sensual kind of love kiss that would be more or less typified by the word *eros*. The word *philia* and its Hebrew equivalent obviously has a rather broad connotation. But now it will be helpful to look at the use of this significant word, *philia*, in the Synoptic Gospels (Matthew, Mark, and Luke) and then in the Gospel of John.

The Synoptic Gospels

Often in the Synoptic Gospels, *philia* can be translated "to prefer, or to place above." Clearly, we are to prefer Jesus and place Him above our relatives (Luke 14:26). As one author has expressed it, "Jesus does not claim for Himself the same measure of love as that given to neighbors but the superabundance of love due to God (Mark 12:30-33) . . . it is one of the strongest expressions of Jesus' self-understanding. Because He is and speaks and acts like God, He wants to be loved like God."[8] These and other such examples can be discovered in the first three books of the New Testament.

The Gospel of John

At times John employed the term to imply, "to love what belongs to or is one's own." But on a higher level, just like in the first three books of the New Testament, in John's gospel, the Lord Jesus Christ demands the unconditional love of His disciples that manifests itself in total commitment (John 14-15, 21). *Philia* certainly means all that.

As already discovered, the idea of friendship is ingredient to the term. In describing Jesus' relationship to Lazarus, our Lord chooses *philia*. What a dramatic portrait of love. *Philia* connotes the kind of love that brought Lazarus from the tomb (John 11). The same basic usage resides in the love Jesus had for the "beloved disciple" in the fourth gospel. This is an instance of the use of the term for a love that chooses and prefers. It expresses the intimacy of a unique relationship of trust, as seen in the beloved disciple's lying on Jesus' breast during the Last Supper. There is even an instance where *philia* serves as a term describing God's special love for His disciples, but then it slips over into the *agape* motif (John 16:27). John also uses the word *philia* in the setting of "friend of the bridegroom" (John 3:29). It shows the close friendship and relationship that John the Baptist felt with the Lord Jesus Christ and his absolute subordination to Him. John did not see himself as the bridegroom, he simply served as the "best man." In the fourth gospel, this would connote the best man's having the most unselfish friendship *(philia)* for the bridegroom. Actually, *philia* becomes a very powerful and significant spiritual term in the hands of John.

Other Uses in the New Testament

The rest of the New Testament likewise uses this interesting word for love. In 1 Corinthians 16:22, the apostle Paul employs the term to say that only those who love the Lord should be invited to participate in the Lord's Supper. At times, Paul uses it as something of a comprehensive word for a sincere attitude of faith focused essentially and exclusively on Jesus Christ. Noteworthy is the fact that the word *philia* can never be found in the erotic sense as *eros* can nor in an egocentric sense as Plato understood it. In like manner, therefore, the kiss of love in the New Testament always denotes essentially what it did in the Old Testament. Derivatives of the term center around the concept of "dearest," "beloved," "friend," with no erotic or egocentric suggestion whatsoever.

The idea of philia as spiritual friendship enjoys quite extensive use in the New Testament. For example, Jesus calls His disciples His friends in Luke 12:4. This does not mean a friendship of absolute equals. As one has put it, "It is the Master and Teacher who is calling His disciples and pupils friends."[9] Flowing from this essential idea in our Lord's use of the word, Jesus looks forward to His friends' future work and their final destiny. That has great implications for Christian service and for the hope of everlasting life.

A negative idea can be attached to the idea of love as friendship. James tells us that to be a friend of this world makes one an enemy of God (James 4:4). So it becomes vitally important where one places one's philia. One cannot be a friend of God and a friend of the world at the same time.

Much more could be said about this intriguing Greek word and its use in the New Testament. But the above should make it clear that many aspects of the qualities of philia love stand out as very Christian, and hence, most important for one's understanding and experience. Therefore, this quality of love should be sought after. At the same time, however, it normally does not connote the final and ultimate sense of true Christian love—as Henry Drummond expressed it: the greatest thing in the world. *Philia*, only when it is used as a synonym for *agape* or Jesus' friendship, attains the final form of God's great expression of love to us—and what He expects in response to Him. Those truths are found in the pungent word *agape*. To that central idea we finally turn.

Agape

We now come to the essence of what Paul wrote in 1 Corinthians 13:13 when he said, "Now abide faith, hope, love, these three; but the greatest of these is love"—*agape*. Plato and the Greeks tragically missed it all with their eros approach. As one scholar declared:

> A brief but emphatic word of warning must here be given against the old but now no longer always harmless misunderstanding by which Plato's Eros is confused with Agape to which Paul dedicates his "Hymn to Love" in 1 Cor. 13 . . . As the latter knew nothing of Eros, so the former knew nothing of Agape.[10]

The implication of the scholar's words makes it clear that there can be no doubt that eros and agape reside in two entirely different spiritual worlds. Moreover, it has become quite obvious that although philia plays a significant role in the Christian experience, agape love is where the primary essence of the love of God can be found. Actually, *agape,* in the vast majority of the cases, connotes a quite different quality of love as even *philia*. One Bible commentator pointed out: "This distinction is so marked that in scores of cases the two words *agapan* and *philien* could not be exchanged."[11] Agape love speaks exclusively of God's quality of love. As we come more and more to realize all that the beautiful term *agape* means in relationship to God and believers, we will understand, as one New Testament scholar expressed it, "how infinitely precious the disciples are in the eyes of Jesus . . . (and) in the eyes of the Father."[12] Therefore, God's kind of love becomes what we must seek above all, for that love never fails. Agape love resides right in the very heart of God Himself and is therefore the love to be relied on and exemplified in one's life. When Paul wrote 1 Corinthians 13, *agape* was the word he used throughout the chapter. It demands a thorough understanding.

The Essence of Agape

How beautiful the agape approach. To capture it in a simple expression, agape must be seen as the fundamental motif of the entire Christian experience. The Christian alone can grasp and experience all it means. Anyone is capable of eros; the redeemed alone love on the agape plane. And it all grows out of God's great love for us, from His grace alone. As one Bible commentator so aptly put it: "Perish the thought of any merit on our part! This word is in accord only with the infinite greatness and magnanimity of him whose delight it is to bestow it."[13]

All this stands as irrevocably true for a number of very important reasons. First, as already stressed, "God is love *[agape]*" (1 John 4:8).

Second, whenever love in any form is attributed to God, whether it be a description of His character or His subsequent actions, the word *agape* is invariably used, save the exceptions in the life of Jesus pointed out earlier. This clearly implies that everything God does emerges out of His great agape love, the expression of His innermost character. The well-known verse John 3:16 stands as the epitome of this principle: "God so loved *[agape]* the world that He gave . . ." God always gives because that constitutes the nature of agape love. Agape love speaks of intelligent, purposeful, *giving* love; for God bestowed the supreme gift when in love He gave Himself in the person of His Son to die for the sins of the world. That quality of love was supremely expressed when Jesus willingly gave of Himself in life, death, and resurrection. Eros knows nothing of that utterly selfless divine love.

Third, the ethical dimension of this love becomes incumbent on all believers. The Lord Jesus Christ said, " 'You shall love the Lord your God with all your heart, and with all your soul, and with all your mind.' This is the great and foremost commandment. The second is like it, 'You shall love your neighbor as yourself.' On these two commandments depend the whole Law and the Prophets" (Matt. 22:37-40). This creates a new kind of love. As has been said:

> Many features of this newness [differentiate] the precept of Jesus from the old law, "Thou shalt love thy neighbor as thyself," which reaches out to all men, even to our enemies. But it is best to abide by the newness which Jesus himself points out: that you keep loving each other "just as I love you." Jesus makes all things new. The newness Jesus has in mind is not strange and startling to the disciples, it has a familiar and a pleasant mien. Jesus has brought a new love into the world, a love that is not only faultless and perfect as love but one that is intelligently bent on salvation for the one loved. Only the disciples know from Jesus what this love is, only they have enjoyed the experience of his love; hence this precept is for them alone—it would be useless to give it to the world. So also this love is to be for 'each other' in the circle of his disciples. It cannot be otherwise, because the tie that binds the disciples of Jesus is a thing apart and

cannot include others. Just as Jesus loves his "little
children," and there is an intimate exchange of love between
him and them, so it is with regard to the exchange of love
between these "little children" themselves.[14]

And Jesus further said, "He who has My commandments and
keeps them, he it is who loves Me; and he who loves Me shall be
loved by My Father, and I will love him, and will disclose Myself
to him" (John 14:21). The ethical and moral implications are deep
and profound. It goes far beyond merely trying to do good and
be a loving person and hoping thereby to find favor with God;
eros can do that. Agape strikes right at the very core of one's being.
The ethical principle of agape love is the "good within itself;" good
because it reflects God's quality of love and good because no place
can be found for self-seeking whatsoever. That goes far beyond
Plato's concept of eros as the "good within itself." God and His
glory alone form the object and goal of agape.

If all of these things be true, as one writer has expressed it:

> We have therefore every right to say that *agape* is the centre
> of Christianity, the Christian fundamental motif *par
> excellence*, the answer to both the religious and the ethical
> question. Agape comes to us as a quite new creation of
> Christianity. It sets the mark on everything in Christianity.
> Without it nothing that is Christian would be Christian. Agape
> is Christianity's own original basic conception.[15]

Herein emerges the essence of it all: God's love rests at the
heart and center of God's very nature and must become the core
of dynamic Christianity for the believer.

A New Life

This fathomless love of God brings about a whole new idea
and motif of what can be seen as meaningful and good in life.

Virtually every aspect of life outside of true Christianity can be more or less characterized by eros, self-centeredness. This does not mean that a person who has not yet come to living faith in Jesus Christ is necessarily a mean, ugly, vindictive person as the world would understand it. They may be very nice and helpful. But the self has never been truly dethroned. Even though people may do benevolent acts and be loving on the surface, such a lifestyle still emerges out of the self and thus ultimately, as the apostle Paul made very clear, leads to death in trespasses and in sin (Eph. 2:1-3). That may sound harsh, but it is true. Eros ultimately spells death.

In Henry Drummond's day, people would talk about the "exceeding sinfulness of sin." We have tended in our culture to forget that fact. We need reminding that God is holy, and sin in His sight is abominable. But thanks be to God for His great love; sin and death do not have the final word. While living an eros lifestyle far from God, there comes to the human heart the wonderful message of the gospel: Christ in love died in our place. And if one will exercise "repentance toward God and faith in our Lord Jesus Christ" (Acts 20:21) and thus dethrone self and turn to God, making Jesus Christ King and Lord, death is destroyed. As one flees to God in true repentance and faith, one receives eternal life. Faith in Christ and His great work of love brings it all to pass. That constitutes salvation, and it means a complete, radical life reorientation. That makes up the agape principle. One writer has put it this way, "It is in Christianity that we first find egocentric religion essentially superseded by theocentric religion."[16] What a radical and revolutionary change this beautiful truth declares. From this complete turn to God, genuine and blessed fellowship with God becomes established, and that truly does exemplify and brings to reality "the good in itself" in one's life.

In the final analysis, life reduces itself to this: We have either an egocentric orientation to our existence or a Christocentric lifestyle. In our essential commitment, we exist either in relationship with ourselves or in relationship with God. The choice is always eros or agape; no middle ground can be found. Jesus said, "He who is not with Me is against Me" (Matt. 12:30). As pointed out earlier, this does not mean that the eros-centered person cannot be religious. To the contrary, many very religious people make an effort to keep the law; however they may understand their religious "law." The radical difference in true Christianity centers in the fact that agape brings one into a dynamic fellowship of *grace* with God Himself, and this makes all the difference in the world. How deep and profound that relationship and fellowship becomes. Lenski expressed it as follows: "The relation between the divine Saviour and the human souls he has saved is a lovely reflection of the supreme relation between the Father and the Son."[17] We become related to Christ as He is related to the Father (John 17:23). Such a thought almost staggers the imagination. As has been said, "It makes all the difference whether we are interested in God as the One who can satisfy all the needs and desires of the ego, or as the sovereign Lord who has absolute authority over the ego."[18] Those who have moved into the agape experience of God in Christ have given the Lord Jesus Christ the place of absolute authority over the ego. *He is Lord!*

It is not incidental that Christianity, properly understood, holds a unique place among the world's religions. No other faith comes close to it philosophically, theologically, historically, or practically. The vast difference rests between agape and eros, faith and works. Jesus Christ has revolutionized the fundamental questions of what constitutes true religion and what thus leads to true ethical, moral living. The rest of this book shall be an attempt to make this increasingly clear—and how to live it out. To put it in the simplest of terms, the difference between agape and eros is not one of degree but of actual kind. Eros love and religion are humanly generated; agape only comes from God in the redemptive grace of Jesus Christ. It makes real sense when John said, "Everyone who loves is born of God and knows God" (1 John 4:7b). What a difference He makes, not only in eternity but in everyday godly living as well. As stated, the ethics of agape are most profound indeed. We need to look afresh at that dimension.

The Ethics of Agape

Anders Nygren has put his finger on the ethical, moral dimensions of agape living when he said:

> If the Commandment of Love can be said to be specifically Christian, as undoubtedly it can, the reason is to be found, not in the commandment as such, but in the quite new meaning that Christianity has given it. The love it requires does not mean the same in a Christian context as it meant (even) in Judaism. To reach an understanding of the Christian idea of love simply by reference to the Commandment of Love is therefore impossible; to attempt it is to move in a circle. We could never discover the nature of Agape, love in the Christian sense, if we had nothing to guide us but the double command: "Thou shalt love the Lord thy God with all thy heart" and "Thou shalt love thy neighbour as thyself." It is not the commandment that explains the idea of Agape, but insight into the Christian conception of Agape that enables us to grasp the Christian meaning of the commandment. We must therefore seek another starting-point.[19]

And what makes up the Christian concept of agape, that starting point, that enables us to grasp and live out the Christian meaning of the great commandment? Paul had it right when he said in Romans 5:5, "The love of God *[agape]* has been poured out within our hearts through the Holy Spirit who was given to us." We shall see this basic, essential principle unfold in far more detail—and glory—in the next chapter as we expand on Henry Drummond's work. But let it be understood right at the outset, agape constitutes the essential motif of Christianity and that love is poured into our hearts by the indwelling Holy Spirit. That makes for godly, ethical living.

By way of summary of all that has been said so far—and hopefully we have plowed and not plodded—God's equality of love revolves around the fact that Jesus does not simply seek to bring us into a new idea or concept of God or to a new theology about the Most High so we can merely contemplate the idea. What Jesus came to bring centers in a new dynamic *fellowship* with God. This radically new element of agape love resides right at the very heart of our entire ethical spiritual life. To use a biblical image, here we find the "new wine." That new wine can never be poured into the old wineskins of striving to keep the Law and be religious hoping to find God and happiness; it only comes about by moving into a living fellowship with the living God, and that means the grace of agape. The very core and orientation of our entire life moves from an ego-centered existence to a Christ-centered life. And that means genuine fellowship with God, as distinguished from all other kinds of so-called "experiences of the Lord." Agape forms the only viable basis of intimacy with God Himself and the subsequent ethical, holy lifestyle.

One more important aspect of the central truth of agape means that we no longer dare ask questions about the "goodness" or "badness" of people whom God sees as objects of His love. When we raise the question, why does God love people of all sorts, only one correct answer rises to the surface: because His very nature is to love in utter, self-giving agape style. He does not love because we strive to be good or not good. God loves us because He does. Therefore, we must not judge others. Jesus said in the Sermon on the Mount, "Do not judge lest you be judged" (Matt. 7:1). This does not mean that Christians are not known by their fruits (Matt. 7:16), it simply states that agape love does not harbor a judgmental spirit. But we never know for certain who truly knows Christ.

Having laid the essential foundation of agape, we need to see more clearly some of the ramifications of just what makes up the content of agape.

The Agape Content

The main features of God's quality of love can be summarized in four basic areas.

First, agape must be grasped as absolutely spontaneous and, as has been said, unmotivated. This becomes clear when we realize how God has loved us, as personified in the incarnation, life, death, resurrection, and glorification of our Lord Jesus Christ. We can look until we wear our eyes out trying to find an explanation as to why God has loved us to that extent. How can we ever explain His utter self-giving? Certainly no ground can be found in us sinful creatures. We are wretched, no matter how we may scale the heights of eros. But, as stressed above, God loves simply because such is His nature. The only ground, therefore, in receiving God's love rests in the fact that God loves in a spontaneous and totally unmotivated manner. When we say that God so loved the world, this is not because of humankind's goodness but because of who God is. And we can say no more.

This unmotivated agape love explains why Jesus consorted with publicans and sinners. It was precisely for these kinds of people that His great love moved Him to come, to seek, and to save. And in the final analysis, we are all these kinds of people apart from Christ; make no mistake, we are all in ourselves publicans and sinners, ego oriented. But the divine love has reached out to us and transformed us by grace through faith (Eph. 2:8-9). Perhaps it can be expressed this way: motivated love is human; spontaneous and unmotivated love is divine. Agape really is the new wine that Jesus spoke of that burst the old wineskins of the Law, of eros. What incredible love God has; what an incredible God!

Second, as implied, agape must be seen as actually indifferent to human values. God's unmotivated love leads to such a conclusion. This principle can be seen when Jesus said He came not to call the righteous but to call sinners (Matt. 9:13). Jesus did a complete reversal of what the egocentric mind demands or expects. Surely, one would think, God must be pleased with people who are moral and displeased with immoral people. In one sense, true enough; but the issue stands that all people are sinners, and when a person realizes there can be no such thing as human righteousness pleasing to God, then one reaches out in faith to embrace the agape of God. We remember the words of the apostle Paul that reinforce this basic truth when he said, "There is none righteous, not even one" (Rom. 3:10). Of course, the question can be raised: Then why do we have the Ten Commandments? Paul likewise answered this query very clearly when he told us that the Law came as a "schoolmaster" (literally a "child conductor") to bring us to Christ (Gal. 3:24 KJV). The Law came to show us that we cannot keep the Law, and therefore, in the sight of God, we are all dead in trespasses and in sins (Eph. 2:1); thus worthy of the judgment of God. But right there the great incredible love of God reaches out to us to rescue and redeem. Agape in this sense must be recognized as indifferent to human values. God saves sinners. We should see our plight and turn to the gracious God of love.

Third, agape always contains a strong creative element. Why do we say that agape comes to us as creative? It is creative because of the fact we *encounter* divine love and thus share in all the creativeness of God Himself. Again Nygren expressed it beautifully when he said:

God does not love that which is already in itself worthy of love, but on the contrary, that which in itself has no worth acquires worth just by becoming the object of God's love. Agape has nothing to do with the kind of love that depends on the recognition of a valuable quality in its object; Agape does not recognise value, but creates it. Agape loves, and imparts value by loving. The man who is loved by God has no value in himself; what gives him value is precisely the fact that God loves him. *Agape is a value-creating principle.*[20]

That is marvelous indeed. How wonderful to realize that God creates us by His great love into a valuable "commodity" in His sight. In ourselves we have no inherent value; but Christ in grace and love creates us such. Thus, He brings us into fellowship with Himself. Because of agape we can now say, "We have peace with God through our Lord Jesus Christ" (Rom. 5:1).

Finally, agape becomes the foundation of a new fellowship with God. This point has already been labored, but it must be repeated once more to see something of the incredible grace that permeates the fellowship-love motif of the New Testament. Love in this sense far exceeds mere "warm and fuzzy" sentimental feelings about God and ourselves. That can be no more than worked up emotionalism. Paul put his finger on the real meaning of it in his prayer for the Ephesians when he prayed:

So that Christ may dwell in your hearts through faith; and that you, being rooted and grounded in love, may be able to comprehend with all the saints what is the breadth and length and height and depth, and to know the love of Christ which surpasses knowledge, that you may be filled up to all the fullness of God (Eph. 3:17-19).

Notice the dual aspect of agape as Paul sets it out in his prayer. The apostle first asks that they may *comprehend*. That makes up the intelligent side of love. And then Paul prays that they may *know*. This word means to know *by experience*. That constitutes the experiential dimension of love. Agape encompasses both. Therefore it is an intelligent love, a truthful love, a tough love. No room can be found for deception about ourselves or others or situations—love tells the full truth.

God's kind of love is intended to be experienced as well as understood. Faith in all Christ is and declares insures that reality, for faith and love cannot be separated. They always go together; one of faith's fruits is love. That brings the experience of peace and meaning to life in Christ. How great an all-encompassing love God has and showers upon us.

We see all this beautifully expressed in the first epistle of John. The apostle wrote, "What we have seen and heard we proclaim to you also, that you also may have fellowship with us; and indeed our fellowship is with the Father, and with His Son Jesus Christ" (1 John 1:3). Agape serves as God's avenue into our lives and ours into His. In this new fellowship of faith and love is found forgiveness, life, and eternity. And make no mistake, agape expressed in Christ's sacrifice is absolutely the exclusive and only way to God. The Lord Jesus Himself said, "I am the way, and the truth, and the life; no one comes to the Father, but through Me" (John 14:6). Therefore, agape must be grasped as the *only* way to fellowship with God the Father. Eros, religious and otherwise, will surely fail. Only Christ can make us children of God, adopted into the divine family. And that answers one of life's basic questions: Who am I? That in turn gives true meaning to life.

What a marvelous concept: God's utter self-giving, unmotivated, glorious, abiding, dynamic, life-changing, fellowship creating, transforming love can be ours. What other adjectives can we find to describe God's love! And we must realize that love is not God; God is love! He is a *Person*, not a principle, who personally loves us. Realize how unfathomable this agape love of God truly is.

Little wonder, therefore, in the light of God's great love for us, that the Lord Jesus said, "And you shall love the Lord your God with all your heart, and with all your soul, and with all your mind, and with all your strength" (Mark 12:30). These words make it obvious that our Lord demands absolute devotion and submission in love to Him because of His love for us. That sets the Christian experience and the Christian ethic apart from the rest of the world. As the Lord Jesus said, "Freely you received, freely give" (Matt. 10:8). The love required of us has its roots in the love manifested by God and must therefore be "spontaneous and unmotivated, uncalculating, unlimited, and unconditional."[21] We love Him "because He first loved us" (1 John 4:19).

Conclusion

Henry Drummond's small but significant exposition of 1 Corinthians 13 implies all these great realities. This explains why he sees love as the greatest thing in the world. But this still leaves us with a very central question: How can we ever love like that? Why do so many professing Christians appear to be almost oblivious of this quality of love? To put it on a very personal plain, Why do all of us so often fail to exhibit agape in all of its beauty and glory as the reflection of God's consistent, constant, selfless love to us? These vital questions must be addressed.

Endnotes

1. C. S. Lewis, *Mere Christianity* (New York: Touchstar Books, 1996), 47.
2. Anders Nygren, *Agape and Eros* (England: S. P. C. K. House, 1932), 172-73.

3. Ibid., 175.
4. Ibid.
5. Ibid., 180.
6. C. S. Lewis, *The Four Loves* (New York: Harcourt Brace Jovanovich, 1960), 56.
7. Gerhard Kittel, ed., *Theological Dictionary of the New Testament*, vol. 9 (Grand Rapids: Eerdmans, 1974), 135.
8. Ibid., 129.
9. Ibid., 163.
10. Nygren, *Agape and Eros*, 31.
11. R. C. H. Lenski, *The Interpretation of St. John's Gospel* (Minneapolis: Augsburg, 1963), 260.
12. Ibid., 1135.
13. Ibid., 868.
14. Ibid., 960.
15. Ibid., 48.
16. Ibid., 46.
17. Ibid., 736.
18. Ibid., 45.
19. Nygren, *Agape and Eros*, 62-63.
20. Ibid., 78.
21. Ibid., 91.

The Holy Spirit: The Author of Love

The love of God has been poured out within our hearts through the Holy Spirit who was given to us.

Romans 5:5

We have now discovered how the Scriptures use the word *love*. We have plowed through the field of the three Greek terms: *eros, philia,* and *agape*. We needed a real overturning of the soil to uncover their beautiful biblical truths if we wished to understand fully what Paul meant when he said, "the greatest of these is love" (1 Cor. 13:13). What have we learned?

First, we have seen that fallen human beings are quite capable of loving in the eros sense. That makes up the essence of a life without Christ, and a frustrating life it can be. As one Bible scholar expressed it so well, "Scripture's intent characterizes us all as beings made of Swiss cheese, full of holes human efforts cannot fill . . . we have not fully taken into account the nature and degree of human falleness."[1]

Second, we have further discovered that in our better hours, even as non-Christians, we can love in some sense on the philia plane. Many great philanthropists, for example, are not Christians. Everyone, to a greater or lesser degree, can express and show a degree of kindness and affection to friends. But of course, when *philia* is used as a Christian virtue—as we discovered in several biblical instances—that becomes quite another matter. It lifts the concept to a high, spiritual plane.

When we come to agape, however, we rise to an entirely new realm. As pointed out, when the Bible speaks of God's love or God loving, the *agape* root is almost invariably used. This means that *agape* describes God's kind and level of love. And what a marvelous sort of love it is. As C. S. Lewis said, "God, who needs nothing, loves into existence wholly superfluous creatures in order that he may love and perfect them."[2] Therefore, any sort of agape love that human beings experience emerges out of God's work of love within. Thus we conclude that only a true believer has any possibility of loving in the agape sense. Not only that—and this is most important—only a Christian who properly *understands how to relate to God in love* can continually experience and express agape. In simplest terms, achieving the agape plane of love by our own strength would be utterly impossible. Yet, the Bible commands us to love by that level at all times, no excuses. Still, it seems we fail so often. How do we resolve the dilemma between the commands of our Lord and the limitations of our humanity?

The Answer

The Bible presents a beautiful answer to our human dilemma. It has already been strongly hinted at. It is so simple, yet so profound. We dare not miss it. Paul said, "God has poured out his love *[agape]* into our hearts by the Holy Spirit, whom he has given us" (Rom. 5:5 NIV). Do you see it? God actually, literally pours His agape love in our hearts by the wonderful indwelling Holy Spirit. What a precious thought! In commenting on the principle of that verse, remember that Drummond pointed out that God pours our love for Him in our hearts by the Holy Spirit (Rom. 5:5). John put it this way: "Love *[agape]* is from God" (1 John 4:7); "We love because He first loved us" (1 John 4:19). That truth contains the key to love. In our own strength we cannot even begin to love God or our neighbor on the agape plane as we are expected—yea, commanded—to do; but God enables us to do so *in His power* by the indwelling presence of the Holy Spirit.

Through the Spirit's inner work, as we properly *relate* to

Him, we ascend to His sphere of love. That is why Thayer, in his Greek-English Lexicon, calls agape a quality of love "enkindled by the Spirit." Paul addresses it as the "love of the Spirit" (Rom. 15:30). That principle presents a quite sublime thought. Therein rests the secret and the resolving of the dilemma. If we strive to love *(agape)* on the basis of human strength, it will spell continual failure. Remember, we are like Swiss cheese—full of holes. Only as God pours agape into our hearts by the Holy Spirit can we attain the greatest thing in the world. We shall see in the next chapter that love is actually the fruit of the Spirit. Professor Drummond had it right when he said, "Christ, the Spirit of Christ, interpenetrating ours, sweetens, purifies, transforms all" (p. 40).

Proper Relations to the Holy Spirit

To be properly related to and in dynamic fellowship with the Holy Spirit serves as the key to loving on the highest plane. If the Holy Spirit alone can generate God's kind of love, it obviously becomes vital that we live in vibrant fellowship with Him so He can thereby create agape in our lives. This opens up the whole scriptural teaching on the Holy Spirit and how the believer lives in fellowship with Him, drawing on all He can be to us and do in us. Space forbids going into this beautiful doctrine in detail; still, several things must be grasped if the Christian would move into a rich relationship with God the Spirit and live the agape life.

All Are Spirit-Possessed

It must first be made very clear that every believer has the Holy Spirit living within them. The Bible abounds in verses that make this reality undeniable. For example, Paul said, "If anyone does not have the Spirit of Christ, he does not belong to Him" (Rom. 8:9b). Of course, there may well be times when a Christian feels that God has departed, but such can never be the case. We must not let any emotional reaction contradict Scripture. All true believers have the promise of being indwelt by the blessed third person of the Trinity—the Holy Spirit of God. Along with Paul, many other biblical writers repeat the promise:

> If you are reviled for the name of Christ, you are blessed, because the Spirit of glory and of God rests upon you (1 Peter 4:14).

> And I will ask the Father, and He will give you another Helper, that He may be with you forever; that is the Spirit of truth, whom the world cannot receive, because it does not behold Him or know Him, but you know Him because He abides with you, and will be in you (John 14:16-17).

Paul caps it off by saying, "Do you not know that you are a temple of God, and that the Spirit of God dwells in you?" (1 Cor. 3:16).

What a rich reality! God dwells within. Jesus said, "If anyone loves Me, he will keep My word; and My Father will love him, and We will come to him, and make Our abode with him" (John 14:23). In commenting on this verse, a Bible scholar said:

> Those who love Jesus will be the "mansions" for the indwelling of the Father and the Son. We may say that this *unio mystica* (mystical union) includes also the Spirit, and in the economy and the cooperation of the three Persons is made possible by the Spirit and mediated by him, since it is his office to implant faith and love in us.[3]

We come into a relationship with the Holy Spirit only through our basic relationship with Jesus Christ.

More

Incontestably, every true believer possesses the Spirit of God. But is there more? Although the wonder of the Spirit's indwelling forms the firm foundation of one's proper stance before the Spirit, the Bible does teach more concerning the believer's fellowship with the third person of the Trinity. To fail to grasp this may mean missing a moving, deep, and abiding experience with God the Spirit, which may account for the fact that we do not always exemplify agape love. Christians can, and often do, slide into an eros syndrome.

What then makes up this "more?" If true Christian love arises solely through the work of the Spirit, then it follows that we must have all of *His fullness* in our lives. That becomes the key to unlocking His treasure-house of love: We must experience the Spirit's fullness. In short, we are to live the *Spirit-filled life*. In a passage quoted earlier, Paul made the principle of the Spirit-filled life very clear when he prayed for believers in Ephesians 3:14-19:

> For this reason, I bow my knees before the Father, from whom every family in heaven and on earth derives its name, that He would grant you, according to the riches of His glory, to be strengthened with power through His Spirit in the inner man; so that Christ may dwell in your hearts through faith; and that you, being rooted and grounded in love, may be able to comprehend with all the saints what is the breadth and length and height and depth, and to know the love of Christ which surpasses knowledge, that you may be filled up to all the fullness of God.

The clear connection between love and "all the fullness of God" stands paramount in the Scriptures. This creates the path to experience the love of Christ. As previously pointed out, Paul used a very pungent word in his prayer concerning the knowing of the love of Christ. Lenski defines it: "The verb *ginosko* (to know) means far more than intellectual knowing. It denotes an inner spiritual realization due to the inner contact of faith with Jesus and the Father."[4] He goes on to tell us that the term means: "to know with love and appropriation as one's very own and to reveal that loving ownership by all corresponding actions."[5] After Paul's beautiful prayer, the apostle built on the truth and admonished the Ephesians believers: "And do not get drunk with wine, for that is dissipation, but be *filled with the Spirit*" (Eph. 5:18, emphasis added). This comes to us as a command; no escaping its demands.

We not only possess the Holy Spirit, but God wants us to be *filled* with His Spirit. In that way alone can our Lord's road to love be traveled. We must walk in all the fullness of God and by faith, trust Him to create agape love within. And that necessitates being constantly overflowing with the Spirit of God. Paul's imperative injunction in Ephesians 5:18 must be interpreted as a continuous action. The apostle literally said, "You *must* be *continually* filled with the Spirit of God." Actually, when we walk daily in all the fullness of the Spirit of Christ, He loves *through us,* manifesting His grace. That's love on the highest plane.

At the same time a multitude of ideas as to what the Spirit-filled life means has sprung up—considerable controversy even surrounds the doctrine. So we delve into this vital truth and ask, What does the Bible and experience teach on this central concept?

The Spirit's Fullness

First, the issue must be raised, Is the concept of the "fullness of the Spirit" built on a solid foundation? Let us start our inquiry from the vantage point of Christian testimony. Many illustrations present a positive affirmation to the question. Take the case of evangelist D. L. Moody, the man who so significantly touched Henry Drummond.

Dwight Lyman Moody stands in the annuls of history as one of God's great servants. In the nineteenth century his effective evangelistic ministry spanned two continents. It has been said of Moody that he put one foot in America, one in England, and shook the western hemisphere for Jesus Christ.

In the earlier days of Moody's Christian service, about all that could be said of him was that he toiled incessantly. God blessed his efforts to a point, but he lacked a true touch of the Holy Spirit to make his life and ministry all our Lord would have it be. Much of his service seemed undertaken in human energy alone. He needed to move into the fullness and power of the Spirit. The journey to God's fullness, however, proved difficult for the zealous young man.

Moody's larger ministry began during the Civil War days in America. He held meetings and distributed gospels and tracts among the soldiers and prisoners of war. He ministered on many leading battlefields. When the hostilities ceased, he returned to Chicago. There he labored in a local Sunday school and with the Young Men's Christian Association. Through his efforts in the Sunday school movement, the international Sunday school lessons had their birth. In 1870 at a YMCA convention Moody first met Ira David Sankey, who became his famous singing partner.

In 1867 Moody traveled to Great Britain. He was an unknown in Britain at the time, but he wanted to hear Charles Haddon Spurgeon, the great English preacher. He also sought to meet George Müller, who had founded on faith a large orphanage at Bristol. We shall be looking more into the life and ministry of Müller in a later chapter.

During that visit, Moody met Mr. Henry Varley, a well-known nineteenth-century evangelist. As they sat together on a bench in a public park in Dublin, Varley said to the American evangelist, "The world has yet to see what God will do with and for and through and in and by the man who is fully consecrated to him."

He said *a man*, thought Moody, he did not say a great man, nor a learned man, nor a smart man, but simply a man. I am a man, and it lies with the man himself whether he will or will not make that full and entire consecration. I will try my utmost to be that man. The first significant step on the journey to fullness had taken place. God honored his commitment.

Moody's hunger for a rich experience of God deepened through the preaching of Henry Moorehouse, another famous English preacher. Moorehouse preached in Moody's church in Chicago soon after Moody returned to America. Moody served as a pastor at the time. For a solid week, Moorehouse spoke every night from the text John 3:16, "For God so loved the world, that He gave His only begotten Son, that whosoever believeth in Him should not perish, but have everlasting life" (KJV). Moorehouse declared the centrality of God's agape love in life and service and salvation. His preaching on the love of God changed Moody's whole approach to evangelism. He came to realize, even before he met Henry Drummond, that God's agape is the greatest thing in the world and must lie at the heart of all evangelism. He made it the hallmark of his preaching; but did he exemplify it in his life?

The year 1871 became a critical year for Moody. He realized how ill-fitted he was, humanly speaking, for his work; he simply did not love on God's level. He began to recognize that he desperately needed the Holy Spirit's power for service and to fill his life with love. This realization was heightened by two elderly ladies who sat on a front pew of his Chicago church every time he preached. At the close of the service, they would say to Moody, "We have been praying for you." "Why don't you pray for the people?" Moody would retort. A bit of old eros pride still had its hold. The ladies would reply, "Because you need the fullness of the Spirit." In relating the incident afterward, Moody stated:

I had the largest congregation in Chicago, and there were many conversions. I was in a sense satisfied. But right along those two godly women kept praying for me, and their earnest talk about anointing for special service set me thinking. I asked them to come and talk with me, and they poured out their hearts in prayer that I might receive the filling of the Holy Spirit. There came a great hunger into my soul. I did not know what it was. I began to cry out as I never did before.

At that time, the great Chicago fire wiped out both Farwell Hall and the Illinois Street Church sanctuary—D. L. Moody's church buildings. Moody traveled to New York City to raise funds for the sufferers of the Chicago fire, but inwardly he kept crying out for God's fullness. The ladies' prayers were about to catch up with him. Moody related:

> My heart was not in the work of begging. I could not appeal. I was crying all the time that God would fill me with his Spirit. Well, one day, in the city of New York—oh, what a day!—I cannot describe it, I seldom refer to it; it is almost too sacred an experience to name. Paul had an experience of which he never spoke for fourteen years. I can only say that God revealed himself to me, and I had such an experience of his love that I had to ask him to stay his hand. I went to preaching again. The sermons were not different; I did not present any new truths, and yet hundreds were converted. I would not now be placed back where I was before that blessed experience if you should give me all the world it would be as the small dust of the balance.

Moody had his life-changing experience; he received God's fullness. Such an account can be demonstrated in principle in the experience of people like Evan Roberts of the Welsh Revival,

John Wesley, Charles Finney, and many other great servants of God, not to mention millions of faithful Christians. But is such an encounter really legitimate?

Is It Legitimate?

To find any answer relative to our Christian experience, we must turn to the Bible. The Scriptures always stand as our final authority. And when we do open God's Word, the answer to our question becomes a resounding yes.

Paul made it clear in the Ephesian epistle. In Acts 1:8 Jesus said, "You shall receive power when the Holy Spirit has come upon you." We find this promise further fortified by our Lord as recorded in Luke's gospel: "I send the promise of my Father upon you; but stay in the city, until you are clothed with power from on high" (Luke 24:49 RSV). And Christ kept His promise:

> When the day of Pentecost had come, they were all together in one place. And suddenly there came from heaven a noise like a violent, rushing wind, and it filled the whole house where they were sitting. And there appeared to them tongues as of fire distributing themselves, and they rested on each one of them. And they were all filled with the Holy Spirit and began to speak with other tongues, as the Spirit was giving them utterance (Acts 2:1-4).

An in-depth look at the giving of the Holy Spirit at Pentecost can help our understanding of the inner work of the Holy Spirit in the believer's experience that elevates them to the agape lifestyle of love and service. Many things should be said about this pivotal passage. It proclaims the centrality of the church's task of world evangelization. Pentecost also reveals vital principles concerning evangelistic methods. Further, tremendous truths about prayer and waiting on God emerge from this climactic event. That dramatic day also demonstrates much about the doctrine of the church. Pentecost equipped the church for its primary work. For the present moment, however, we will confine ourselves to observing only two vital principles relative to the theme of Christian love and the Spirit's fullness.

Pentecost Principles

First, on the Day of Pentecost all believers in the Lord Jesus Christ received the Holy Spirit and His fullness as God's gift (Acts 2:38). Although the disciples had experiences in and by the Spirit of God prior to that day (for example, see John 20:22), on the Day of Pentecost the climax of receiving all that the Spirit is to be for believers culminated and set the continuing pattern. As emphasized earlier, since that dramatic hour, whenever people put their faith in Jesus Christ as Lord and Savior, they immediately receive the gift of the Spirit (Acts 2:38).

Second, as these early believers experienced the full gift of the Holy Spirit, they also received an infilling of God's power. As pointed out in the *American Commentary,* these first faithful followers had "a reception from the Spirit of extraordinary powers, in addition to sanctifying grace." They received everything God has for believers in the work of the Spirit. That makes up the essential biblical outline. The "age of the Spirit" had arrived. From then on Jesus Christ would continue His ministry by His Spirit through the church.

This particular passage should not be pushed to extremes, however. Some have read too much into these verses, failing to realize that Pentecost stands as something unique in God's dealings with the church. That divine outpouring constituted of God's giving His Spirit to His people in the full sense (Acts 2:17). On that day, the Holy Spirit came to indwell and fill *all* believers for the first time. Thus, it became a singular epic in the life of the church. In that sense it can no more be repeated than the cross of Christ or the glorious resurrection and ascension of our Lord. Yet at the same time, the passage surely implies that a Christian should have an ongoing abiding experience of the Holy Spirit's fullness as well as knowing that Christ lives in one's heart. God wants Christians to be conscious of the Holy Spirit's infilling along with the fact that He lives within. Pentecost poignantly teaches that principle.

Other Scriptural Experiences

Truths concerning the Spirit-filled life emerge with increasing frequency in subsequent passages in Acts. We read in Acts 4:31, "And when they had prayed, the place where they had gathered together was shaken, and they were all filled with the Holy Spirit, and began to speak the word of God with boldness." Here Luke relates that the disciples who had shared in Pentecost again experienced an infilling of the Holy Spirit. Note that these believers already had the Holy Spirit in their lives. Furthermore, they had been filled with the Holy Spirit prior to the events recorded in Acts 4. But persecution had come upon the church. God, therefore, met their immediate need by granting them a fresh infilling of the Spirit. The obvious implication is that Christians need both the possession and the *constant* filling of the power of God's Spirit. People ought to be led to seek the continual fullness of the Spirit as well as the abiding gift of eternal life (Acts 2:37-39). How will they ever love and serve Christ effectively if they do not? The Spirit alone generates agape in believers.

The Example of Jesus

As could be expected, Jesus lived His entire life in the fullness of the Holy Spirit—and how He loved, even unto death. All He said and did was directed by and permeated with the Holy Spirit. John put it this way: "For the one whom God sent speaks authentic words of God—and there can be no measuring of the Spirit given to *him*" (John 3:34 PHILLIPS). Jesus always exemplified the fullness of the Holy Spirit (Luke 4:1). Christ being our example in all things, we should attempt to emulate Him in His relationship to the Spirit of God.

Space forbids delving into numerous other New Testament passages. Suffice it to say that the Bible literally abounds in examples regarding the Spirit-filled life (see Luke 1:15, 41, 67; Acts 6:3; 7:55; 8:17; 9:17; 10:44, 46; 11:15-16, 24). As far as the Bible is concerned, the overwhelming weight of the Word of God fully supports the theme that being filled with the Holy Spirit constitutes a valid, vital experience. Thus, if we take the Bible seriously—and we must—we cannot sidestep the fact that God intends for all His people to be Spirit-filled Christians.

The Testimony of Church History

Since the Spirit-filled life is a biblically based concept, we should expect to see it surface throughout the entire course of church life. When delving into the experiences of God's loving servants through the ages, constant references to the reality of the Spirit-filled life can be discovered. D. L. Moody's experience is just one link in a long historical chain.

The early church fathers—Origen, Jerome, Ambrose, and others—talked much about the work of the Spirit in the believer's life. As the years of God's dealings with His people unfolded, giants of the Christian faith emphasized the theme. Leaders like Savonarola, Fénelon, George Fox, Madam Guyon, John Bunyan, John Wesley, George Whitefield, and a multitude of others give strong witness to the necessity of being rightly related to the Holy Spirit of God.

The eighteenth century saw a fresh emphasis on this theme. No person in those days was more godly or significantly used by the Spirit than young David Brainerd. His testimony of the Spirit-filled life stands as a classic. Biographer Lawson tells us:

> Brainerd, the consecrated missionary, endured almost incredible hardships while laboring among the American

Indians; but he lived so close to God that his life has been an inspiration to many. His biography was written by Jonathan Edwards, was revised by John Wesley, and influenced the life of Dr. A. J. Gordon more than any other book outside the Bible.

Such intense longings and prayers after holiness as we read of in the journals of Brainerd are scarcely recorded anywhere else. "I long for God, and a conformity to His will, an inward holiness, ten thousand times more than for anything here below," says he. On October 19, 1740, he wrote: "In the morning, I felt my soul *hungering and thirsting after righteousness.* In the forenoon, while I was looking on the sacramental elements, and thinking that Jesus Christ would soon be 'Set forth crucified before me,' my soul was filled with light and love, so that I was almost in an ecstasy; my body was so weak I could hardly stand. I felt at the same time an exceeding tenderness, and most fervent love towards all mankind; so that my soul, and all the powers of it seemed, as it were, to melt into softness and sweetness. This love and joy cast out fear, and my soul longed for perfect grace and glory."

Many were the manifestations of the Spirit in his meetings and during his numerous seasons of fasting and prayer and longings for holiness of life. He seems to have risen above the things of this world to a remarkable degree. In his journal of March 10, 1743, he says: "I felt exceeding dead to the world and all its enjoyments: I was ready to give up life, and all its comforts. Life itself appeared but an empty bubble; the riches, honors, and enjoyments of it extremely tasteless. I longed to be entirely *Crucified* to all things here below. . . . It was my meat and drink to be holy, to live to the Lord, and die to the Lord. And I then enjoyed such a heaven, as far exceeded the most sublime conceptions of an unregenerate soul; and even unspeakably beyond what I myself could conceive at another time."[6]

That depth of dedication and love can only come by the Holy Spirit and the fullness of His love.

During the nineteenth century, another surge of interest in the Spirit-filled life emerged. A close companion of D. L. Moody, Dr. R. A. Torrey, a very able Bible teacher and preacher, gave his testimony in these words:

> Take my own experience. I had been a minister for some years before I came to the place where I saw that I had no right to preach until I was definitely baptized with the Holy Ghost. I went to a business friend of mine and said to him in private, "I am never going to enter my pulpit again until I have been baptized with the Holy Spirit and know it or until God tells me to go."[7]

Charles H. Spurgeon, no doubt the greatest of all Victorian preachers, on one occasion quoted Luke 11:13 in a sermon: "If ye then, being evil, know how to give good gifts unto your children, how much more shall your heavenly Father give the Holy Spirit to them that ask him?" (KJV). Spurgeon then cried out to the eager congregation:

> O, let us ask Him at once with all our hearts. Am I not so happy as to have in this audience some who will immediately ask? You that are the children of God—to you is this Promise specially made. Ask God to make you all the Spirit of God can make you, not only a satisfied believer who has drunk for himself, but a useful believer who overflows his neighborhood with blessing.

This emphasis did not end with the closing of the nineteenth century, the era that historian Kenneth Scott Latourete called "The Great Century." The twentieth century gives its witness to the theme. As a case in point, in Texas a man of God was preaching at a large rally on the subject of the Spirit-filled life. At the climax of his message he said, "I do not care what you call it, the infilling, the baptism, the second blessing, or whatever. The issue is, have you experienced it?" This statement of the preacher may not be exactly *theologically* precise; probably the preacher should have stated it in more biblical terms and called it the "filling." But what he wanted his hearers to understand centered on the vital importance of an all-out commitment to Jesus Christ and the touch of God's fullness. We must face that question if we aspire to love on God's level as He commands us. Remember that God's love is poured into our hearts by the Holy Spirit alone. So the issue becomes, Are we living in the fullness of the Spirit of God? Few biblical truths stand out quite as pressing as this probing query: Are we living the agape life? We must never forget such is Christ's command (Mark 12:29-31).

The Obvious Conclusion

The necessity of the Spirit-filled life should now be firmly established. Several vital reasons make it clear why it means so much to our practical, everyday Christian lives.

First, a healthy Christian experience depends on the fullness of the Spirit. This stands true for several reasons; not the least important being the fact that only the Spirit-filled believer can know the constant, conscious presence of Jesus Christ. Although our Lord never leaves His people, to be vividly *conscious* of His presence, one must be filled with the life and love of Jesus. Griffith Thomas, a British scholar, states: "The only true immanence of God is the presence of Christ by the Holy Spirit in the heart and life of the believer. . . . It is in relation to the Holy Spirit that the Christian doctrine of God meets the deepest human need."[8] In other words, the Holy Spirit makes the divine immanence and love an experiential and dynamic reality, not mere emotionalism.

This does not necessarily mean that one is *always*

consciously and emotionally aglow with God. One need not be constantly overwhelmed with the Spirit's presence. Every Christian has dry seasons. We all have our dark night of the soul. When this occurs, the hour for stronger faith has arrived. After all, we "walk by faith, not by sight" (2 Cor. 5:7). If God grants us to bask in the sunshine of Christ's conscious presence, the Lord should be thanked for the warming experience. If circumstances, trials, or difficulties cast a shadow of gloom across life's path and God's hand seems hard to find, then the walk of faith becomes vital. At such a time, regardless of feelings, one simply claims the promise of His presence. God has said, "I will never desert you, nor will I ever forsake you" (Heb. 13:5). And that is enough. And we do well to remember what Charles Spurgeon said: "Grace grows best in the winter." So keeping one's subjective feelings rooted in the foundation of the Word of God, we simply walk by faith, knowing that by His Spirit He is always present, regardless of how we may feel at the moment. Our spirit hungers for this reality; and that kind of reality the Holy Spirit alone can give.

Second, the Holy Spirit not only makes the divine immanence real, He enables Christians to live a holy life. The Bible sets forth the concept of personal holiness repeatedly (for example, 2 Cor. 7:1; 1 Thess. 4:7; and Heb. 12:14). To talk about holy living may sound somewhat archaic today, but personal holiness is far from an outmoded idea in the Bible. What constitutes holy living? Living a holy life simply means developing a lifestyle that is yielded, pleasing to God, separated from sin, and totally Christlike. This powerfully impacts a watching world. As Robert Murray McCheyne, the great Scottish pastor, said, "My people's greatest need is *my* personal holiness." Only the Holy Spirit can create holiness in us and move us through eros to philia and on to agape. Remember, God said, "Be holy, for I am the LORD your God" (Lev. 20:7). God is holy (Isa. 6:1-12); we are to be likewise.

Third, the importance of the Spirit-filled life directly relates to growth in Christian maturity. Much needs to be said concerning the theme, but a later chapter will be devoted to this issue. Spirit-filled, maturing Christians mean a Spirit-filled, growing, revived church. How desperately the world needs to see that quality in a congregation. They want to see the love of Christ radiating out from the body of Christ. They have a right to expect that.

In light of all that has been said, biblically and historically and experientially, it becomes unmistakably clear that God fully expects *all* believers to be filled with the Holy Spirit, experiencing and demonstrating Christ's love. That alone makes personal Christianity vital and alive and loving and serviceable.

Yet a mere casual look at contemporary Christianity demonstrates that considerable confusion persists on the vital subject of the Spirit-filled life. Therefore, before going any further, it should prove beneficial to deal with some of the current misconceptions that surround the principle. So many false ideas have grown up around the theme that many sincere Christians have been put off by the obvious error and excess. But we must not miss a blessing because of others who have warped the truth. Let's not throw out the baby with the bath water. So we begin by graciously, but honestly, attempting to clear away some of the underbrush that has sprung up and invaded this beautiful garden of spiritual truth.

Some Necessary Corrections

The first weed to be uprooted centers in the concept that when believers are filled with the Spirit they enter a state of absolute sinless perfection. This "experience" is called by some a "second work of grace." The exponents of this approach describe a traumatic event, similar to the conversion experience, that blasts one into an orbit of perfection thus precluding the believer's ever sinning again. This obviously cannot be squared with what John tells us in his first epistle. He says that if we embrace sinless perfection, we fall into simple self-deception (1 John 1:8). To hold that one never can sin is actually to call God a liar (1 John 1:10). We must wait for heaven for that level of perfection. Even Paul said he had not yet attained it all (Phil. 3:12).

Some feel that the fullness of the Spirit must always be accompanied by a particular gift of the Spirit. Usually the more spectacular gifts, such as tongues, get top billing. Let me illustrate with a personal experience: One night a friend, a very dedicated layman, called at our home. He had brought along a fellow layman whom I had never met. As we fellowshipped together, this new acquaintance asked me if I had ever been filled with the Holy Spirit. I told him, as unassumingly as possible, that I definitely had. He apparently did not expect such a positive answer. Then he asked, "Well, have you ever experienced the infilling with tongues?" "No," I replied, "God has not seen fit to bestow that particular gift on me." He then said, "But you *should* seek the Spirit with tongues."

I appreciated the man's zeal, grateful for his concern that all Christians become Spirit-filled. His error centered in the fact that he failed to understand what the apostle Paul decidedly declared to the Corinthian believers. Paul told them in unequivocal terms that God gives specific gifts, "as He wills" (1 Cor. 12:11) and that not everyone will have all the gifts (1 Cor. 12:28-30). In the bestowal of His gifts, the Holy Spirit creates a body, unified and diverse. It would be a rather strange body if all had, say, the gift of tongues. The body would be no more than one big tongue and not a normal body at all. In a later chapter we shall look at the gifts of the Spirit in considerable detail.

In the third place, there are those who advocate that being filled with the Holy Spirit must invariably be a very emotional experience. That growth of underbrush must be eradicated.

True, being filled with all the fullness of God can be quite emotional. It certainly was for Moody, Brainerd, and others. Religious emotions cannot be condemned in themselves. They can be God-given and a source of great blessing, but we must not embrace the error of insisting that being Spirit-filled *invariably* results in a great emotional upheaval. That can soon degenerate into simple emotionalism. And a world of difference exists between legitimate emotional reactions to spiritual experiences and simply drumming up religious feelings. After all, every believer in Christ has become a unique individual and thus reacts differently to various stimuli. For example, some have a moving emotional reaction at conversion. Others do not. We all recognize it as an error to insist on a certain emotional response to the gospel. The same principle applies to the Spirit-filled life. A radically changed and deeply loving life is what *truly* counts. It resides primarily in the *will*, not the emotions. It is not "how high you jump" when God fills you with His Spirit that matters; rather, what concerns our Lord is how straight you walk in love when you come down to earth.

A fourth false growth demanding uprooting declares that the more one subdues "self," the more God *automatically* fills one with His Spirit. This approach can subtly sidetrack a needy, hungry Christian from coming to a moment of crisis when once and for all he or she yields to God and by faith claims the infilling of the Spirit. It can even thrust one on the basis of the Law and striving in our own strength to love and be holy. A definite reaching out in faith for God's fullness must be exercised. Of course, it may be possible to yield to God rather unconsciously, but such an experience is rare. We normally know when we make any in-depth decision. A profound moving of our will is usually a conscious act. Yielding to God's absolute will is a momentous decision. Therefore, becoming obedient to God's will with a look of faith emerges as central in bringing one into the Spirit-filled life.

We should never be selfish in our seeking. Striving for the Spirit's fullness for self-centered reasons can be tragic—that would be to slip back into the old eros lifestyle. The blessings of God must never be sought for any shallow, personal end. God does not give the Spirit's fullness that we may be thought of as first-class Christians while we view others as inferior. Nor should leaders seek the fullness so they will be known as great leaders or powerful preachers. Not only that, the Spirit's fullness should never be desired so that one can indulge in a retreat from reality and live in some antiseptic, ethereal false realm of the Spirit that inhibits one from coming to grips with the blood, sweat, and tears of this world. Real Christian love thrusts us into that suffering world to meet needs. God wants to be real to us, but not for the purpose of indulgence and misguided spirituality. *The glory and service of Jesus Christ becomes the only ultimate and legitimate goal in striving for God's fullness.* This constitutes the only motive our Lord honors.

Biblical Terminology

Before passing to the more positive presentation of the principle of the Spirit-filled life of love, it will be well to pause briefly and put our terminology on a firm biblical basis; error in terminology can bring about error in thought, if not in actions. Earlier in this chapter the incident was related of a Texas preacher who said it does not matter what you call the experience so long as you experience it. In a sense, that is correct; better to have the right experience with the wrong expression of it than vice versa. Yet, it is best to keep our terminology scriptural, not to be rigid or wooden in approach, but to be biblically accurate. That can help save us from pitfalls.

This Christian lifestyle has been called the "infilling of the Spirit," the "baptism in the Spirit," the "second blessing," a "second work of grace," and so on. At the outset, terms such as second blessing and a second work of grace can be summarily dismissed. These words and expressions and the concept they imply cannot be found in the Bible. Being filled with the Spirit means far more than a second blessing. Remember, Paul's admonition to the Ephesians in 5:18 declares, "be *[continually]* filled with the Spirit." Never does the Bible present the filling as a once and for all experience, a second blessing only. Rather, what describes it best is a *Christian lifestyle*. And to speak of a second work of grace is erroneous; every blessing God gives emerges out of His fathomless grace. Without daily grace, we are doomed.

The terms *infilling* and *baptism* are scriptural, however. Can a distinction be drawn between these two words? It seems sensible not to press a demarcation too far. At times the terms appear to be used synonymously in the Bible. In the bulk of scriptural references, however, the Bible does draw a line. The term *baptism by the Spirit* usually refers to the primary experience of being baptized by the Spirit into the body of Christ at the time of conversion (e.g., Matt. 3:11; Acts 1:5; 1 Cor. 12:13). Baptism in the Spirit speaks normally of that initial reception of the Spirit of God at conversion, although this no doubt should be a time of filling with the Spirit as well.

The biblical writers commonly employ the expression *filled with the Spirit* to describe the experience of believers who walk in surrender and faith in Christ, trusting God daily for His fullness. That is, it speaks of those who have been baptized with the Spirit at conversion and continually seek the Spirit's infilling. By filling the believer with the Holy Spirit, God equips His people for service, ministry, and godly living (see Acts 4:8, 31; 6:5; 7:55) and enables them to bear the "fruit of the Spirit" that centers in love, as we shall see (Gal. 5:22). Again, it seems wise to guard against being too legalistic on this point. Men like Charles G. Finney, R. A. Torrey, and Martyn Lloyd-Jones tended to use the terms interchangeably. It is best to follow the scriptural pattern. This avoids confusion and practical error.

The Real Meaning

The positive side of the truth must now be presented. What does it actually mean to be filled with the Holy Spirit, and how does one go about experiencing it, thus moving into the agape love life? The essence of the concept can best be seen in Paul's oft-quoted admonition: "be [continually] filled with the Spirit" (Eph. 5:18). This verse implies several essential truths.

First of all, we are "leaky vessels," and we need a daily, fresh infilling of God's Spirit to remain overflowing with His presence and power. As often stressed, the proper spiritual stance revolves around our walk with Christ, constantly coming to Him as to a full fount, readying ourselves to be made full and running over with His blessed Holy Spirit. This is what Jesus meant when He said, "If any man is thirsty, let him come to Me and drink. He who believes in Me, as the Scripture has said, 'From his innermost being shall flow rivers of living water'" (John 7:37–38). Christians should be a perpetual source of God's marvelous blessings of love.

Furthermore, times arise when one must ask God for a special infilling to meet some specific task. These experiences have been called "anointings" or "unction" for special service and ministry. The fullness of the Spirit should be seen as more or less a constant reality. The anointing is more momentary and unique. The anointing that Jesus received for His messianic task (Acts 10:38) stands as a classic case in point. This approach is especially prominent in the Old Testament view of the Spirit's work. It implies special outpourings, or anointings, for differing tasks. This aspect of the Spirit-filled life can be seen in instances such as Samuel's anointing David so that his role as king of Israel might be adequately fulfilled (1 Sam. 16:13). We all need this sort of touch of the Spirit. Situations arise in which God desires to use us in a very unusual way. That becomes the time for an anointing, an unction of the Spirit. Most of us have seen this aspect of the Spirit's work in action. For example, when someone is declaring God's Word, it seems that at times a great outpouring of the Spirit descends. All are caught up in the glory of God. Prayer for these special anointings in the will of God is in order. We should on occasion seek a special outpouring of agape love in our lives to meet some need in people's lives. But again, one must not be legalistic in terminology. There are times when the Bible calls this phenomenon "filled with Spirit," as when Peter addressed the leaders of Israel (Acts 4:8).

Therefore, the Christian experience of the indwelling Holy Spirit can be positively summarized as follows: As we walk in the light as He is in the light, continually cleansed by His blood, we come to Him regularly for the infilling of His wonderful Holy Spirit, thus finding life overflowing with divine power and agape love. And at times in God's sovereign purpose, He even gives us an unusual unction of power for service. This constitutes our Father's marvelous way of making us effective in life and service to the glory of Jesus Christ *enabling us to love on an agape plane*. Now we must ask, how does it all come about?

How to Be Filled with the Spirit

Five simple principles, already implied, should answer the fundamental question of how to become a Spirit-filled believer. They form the spiritual exercise to experience the Spirit-filled, loving life. No spiritual legalism should be deduced from these principles they are simple guidelines to move us in the direction of the Spirit's fullness.

Acknowledge

First, there must be an *acknowledgment* of need. If we feel satisfied with our present spiritual state, little progress will be made in the things of God. The Lord Jesus Christ said, "Blessed are those who hunger and thirst for righteousness, for they shall be satisfied" (Matt. 5:6). If we have no real hunger for God or what He has for believers who are seeking, we should ask Him to create such a desire in us. Much surrounds us to move us in that direction. Tragic situations abound all over the world that cry out to be met in Christ's name. We cannot even begin to meet those needs in our own strength; we must have God's love poured into us by the Holy Spirit. The Psalmist expresses the heart of the earnest Christian: "As the deer pants for the water brooks, So my soul pants for Thee, O God. My soul thirsts for God, for the living God; When shall I come and appear before God?" (Ps. 42:1-2). We must continually acknowledge our need, especially our need to love.

Abandon

After God has been able to create something of a genuine hunger and thirst for His love, and having acknowledged one's need, the next imperative step centers in *abandoning* all conscious sins. To make a 100 percent break with all known sin stands out as absolutely necessary. Do not mistake this for sinless perfection. That error has already been abundantly exposed. The issue is, we can make a break with every *known* evil. We must strive to be able to say with Paul, "So I always take pains to have a clear conscience toward God and toward men" (Acts 24:16 RSV). We absolutely must come to grips with our conscious sins and confess them—one by one by name—before God (1 John 1:9). And we should also ask God's forgiveness for sins of which we may not even be aware (Ps. 19:12). That keeps our fellowship with our Lord in good order.

Is this asking too much? Hardly! The Bible says, "If I regard wickedness in my heart, the Lord will not hear" (Ps. 66:18). Sin, unforsaken and unconfessed, severs fellowship with God (1 John 1:6). One can hardly have Christ's fullness in one hand and grasp known sin in the other. Fullness and rebellion are totally incompatible in the believer. Love for Christ moves us to true, continual confession before God—and to put things right if we have sinned against anyone and lost fellowship with them.

Jesus said, "If therefore you are presenting your offering at the altar, and there remember that your brother has something against you, leave your offering there before the altar, and go your way; first be reconciled to your brother, and then come and present your offering" (Matt. 5:23-24).

That too becomes essential for God's fullness. We shall see more of this principle in the next chapter.

Abdicate

The next exercise centers in *abdicating* the throne of one's heart. In the final analysis, we always face one basic issue: Will I control my own life or will I truly make Jesus the Lord of all? We cannot escape, we are forced to decide one way or the other. God's Word speaks very plainly on this point. Remember the principle: The Holy Spirit comes to "those who obey Him" (Acts 5:32). Jesus must be King. We are to love God with our total being; and that means a surrendered will, enthroning Jesus Christ as Lord of life.

Many Christians seem unwilling to make such an in-depth commitment. Why? Perhaps we feel apprehensive that such a decision will force us into becoming less of a real person. To give up ourselves to another—even God—may appear to destroy something of our essential freedom and personhood. Nothing could be further from the truth. The devil's deception produces that reaction. Actually, we become real persons when we yield to Jesus Christ. One is only truly "free" as the Son of God makes one free (John 8:36). We "find" our lives when we "lose" them for Jesus (Matt. 10:39).

We also may fear that God will ask some terrible thing of us if we yield ourselves to His control. Never forget, however, that our Father God is love. Understanding and compassion rest at the heart of our Lord. He only wants the very best for His children. His will alone brings fulfillment and meaning and reality to life.

Still, it seems far from easy to yield one's self to Jesus Christ—even realizing all these truths. But God will help us even here. For example, one day a man came to a minister of the gospel and related that he wanted to be filled with the Holy Spirit, but he just could not bring himself to yield to the absolute lordship of Jesus Christ. The preacher asked him if he were willing to be yielded to God if the Holy Spirit would give him the strength to surrender. The man replied he did not know. The minister then asked, "Are you willing for God to make you willing?" The man replied, "Yes, I'm willing for that." So the man of God pointed the inquirer to 1 John 5:14-15: "And this is the confidence which we have before Him, that if we ask anything according to His will He hears us. And if we know that he hears us in whatever we ask, we know that we have obtained the requests which we have asked from Him." Knowing it was surely God's will that the man be willing to commit all to Christ, they prayed that God would make the seeker willing to be made willing to yield himself to the lordship of Jesus. They shared in mutual prayer, claiming God's promise that He would hear. The power of Christ's love entered the inquirer's life, and he found that he could willingly present himself without reservation to God and seek the fullness of the Spirit. Perhaps that is where most of us must begin. Such a sincere prayer will surely be divinely honored. The Father will hear and enable us to make Jesus Christ our *Lord* in the fullest sense.

Ask

Fourth, after acknowledging need, abandoning sin, and abdicating control of our lives, we simply *ask* God to fill us with His Spirit. Jesus said, "If you then, being evil, know how to give good gifts to your children, how much more shall your heavenly Father give the Holy Spirit to those who ask Him!" (Luke 11:13). God deeply desires His hungry-hearted children to come into His presence by prayer and ask Him for this work of the Spirit. He waits for hungry, cleansed, yielded Christians to ask Him for the Spirit's fullness. This strikes at the heart of the crisis moment—and the continuing discipline.

Accept

Finally, having asked, we now *accept* the gift of fullness by faith and thank God for His goodness. We need not necessarily pray long and agonizingly. God honors acceptance by faith. We receive salvation by faith and do not ask for any sign or particular feeling that God has genuinely saved us; so also we claim by faith the infilling of the Holy Spirit. We rest in His promise.

This can be something of a problem, however. It often takes some time to see the reality of simple faith in receiving the fullness of the Holy Spirit. This author's heart had been hungry for God's fullness. The Holy Spirit had been at work on the issue for a protracted period in my life. One night as a growing crisis developed, I determined: *I will not go to bed until I am assured that I have been filled with the Holy Spirit, even if it takes all night.* Alone with God, I determined to get the matter settled once and for all—and at all cost.

Many factors in providential experiences had brought me to that critical point. I had thought, prayed, discussed, and read about the theme for months, even years. Now I was determined. At any cost, I wanted my life filled with God and His love. Yet pray as I would, the heavens seemed as brass; no answer came. I suppose in my zeal and lack of understanding I expected certain manifestations of the Spirit's fullness. I had read about the great spiritual experiences of significant people, but it was not happening to me as to Moody or others. So I prayed and prayed.

Soon I found myself getting into something of a state. My experience seemed to be empty; in fact, I was not having any experience at all as far as I could sense it. At that moment, my eyes fell on a simple statement in R. A. Torrey's little book, *The Holy Spirit: Who He Is and What He Does*. He said that if one had paid the full price of surrender and confession, all one had to do was simply claim the promise. He emphasized the mistake of looking for a great emotional experience. Perhaps that is why I have so often stressed that principle in this chapter. Suddenly the light dawned. The simple truth swept over me like "rivers of living water." *That's it,* I exclaimed to myself. The emotional response is irrelevant. Of course, this does not mean that we stand like stoic statues and repress all emotions. Make no mistake, the Christian should have passion, but the passion is for Jesus and His fullness—and for His glory. Christians do feel deeply about what truly matters. But as long as we are surrendered, God will surely meet our need. How refreshing! The Spirit-filled life waits for the receiving by God's yielded, trusting people. We should thank Him for His marvelous blessing of filling us with the Holy Spirit.

So I closed my books and Bible, thanked the Father for His fullness, and went to bed. Now, every day, I practice the five simple disciplines outlined above and by faith walk with God. That was my beginning of a true walk in the agape of God.

And what God has done for me and multitudes of His people, He can and will do for you. The Spirit-filled life of love stands waiting for every believer to claim. Continually yielded, cleansed, filled! That is how one loves. Love comes by the inner work of the loving Holy Spirit. That is why Paul urged believers to "love in the Spirit" (Col. 1:8). Daily walking in His fullness lays the foundation for God's love to be poured into our hearts. That becomes the path from eros to agape. That is basic Christianity. And that is the greatest thing in the world.

Endnotes

1. Bryan Chapell, *Christ-Centered Preaching: Redeeming the Expository Sermon* (Grand Rapids: Baker, 1994), 291.
2. C. S. Lewis, *The Four Loves* (New York: Harcourt Brace Jovanovich, 1960), 176.

3. R. C. H. Lenski, *The Interpretation of St. John's Gospel* (Minneapolis: Augsburg, 1963), 1011.

4. Ibid., 774.

5. Ibid., 736.

6. James Gilchrist Lawson, *Deeper Experiences of Famous Christians* (Anderson, Ind.: Warner Press, 1911), 346.

7. Ibid., 373-74 (edited).

8. W. H. Griffith Thomas, *The Holy Spirit of God*, 3d ed. (Grand Rapids: Eerdmans, 1955), 196-97.

4

Love Is a Fruit

By this is My Father glorified, that you bear much fruit.

John 15:8

Wonderful indeed is the thought that the gracious Spirit of God, who Himself has been poured into our hearts, becomes the great Enabler so we can keep our Lord's command to love. And far from a mere thought, it is a blessed reality.

If such be the case, a question arises: How does the Holy Spirit actually effect such a work in our lives? The Bible heralds the answer in clear tones. Again from the pen of the apostle Paul, we read, "The fruit of the Spirit is love, joy, peace, patience, kindness, goodness, faithfulness, gentleness, self-control; against such things there is no law" (Gal. 5:22-23). In basic terms, love must be understood as the *fruit* of the Spirit. The humanly impossible responsibility to love on the agape plane becomes realized as the Holy Spirit blossoms out in our lives and increasingly bears that glorious fruit within.

When we speak of the fruit of the Spirit, this does not imply that the Spirit-filled believer who would walk in the love of Christ is merely passive and the Holy Spirit automatically bears the fruit. Although the work unfolds primarily under the authorship and power of the Spirit of God, the believer plays a very active role in intelligently cooperating with Him that His fruit might be made manifest. This chapter, therefore, will attempt to set forth not only how the Holy Spirit operates in bearing fruit, but also what those beautiful manifestations of His grace actually become in practical living. We will also deal with our responsibility by looking at themes such as abiding in Christ so as to make these principles a glowing reality.

So we set out on the wonderful venture. As the Spirit of God works within and as we intelligently cultivate the ground that He might flourish in His fruit-bearing grace, life takes on a ringing tone of the love of Christ. Consequently, we realize on a down-to-earth level what it means to experience the beauty of the greatest thing in the world.

The Beauty of Love and Holiness

Madame Guyon, a deeply spiritual French Christian, said:

> I had a deep peace which seemed to pervade the whole soul, and resulted from the fact that all my desires were fulfilled in God. . . . I desired nothing but what I now had, because I had firm belief that, in my present state of mind, the results of each moment constituted the fulfillment of the Divine purposes. . . . I had no will but the Divine will. One characteristic of this higher degree of experience was a sense of inward purity. . . . My mind had such a oneness with God, such a unity with the Divine nature, that nothing seemed to have power to soil it and to diminish its purity.

That's beautiful. Loving saints of God always develop a lovely, God-conscious lifestyle. The agape life and a holy life blend into one. All God ever attempts to effect in any Christian's experience centers in enabling one to grow into the beauty and love of Jesus. Paul put it this way: "This is the will of God, your sanctification" (1 Thess. 4:3). J. B. Phillips translates the apostle: "God's plan is to make you holy." The Holy Spirit's dynamic design for our lives revolves around growing in love and attractive consecration. That constitutes the "much fruit" that Jesus spoke of that we are to bear to God's glory (John 15:8). God places the standard before us; our part is to grow up to meet it. Bearing the "fruit of the Spirit" thus becomes a vital aspect of the entire Christian experience of love.

The Heart of It All

In Galatians 4:19 Paul pleaded, "Oh, my dear children, I feel the pangs of childbirth all over again till Christ be formed within you" (Phillips). In this passage the pathos of Paul surges to the surface as he yearns over these early Christians, pleading that "Christ be formed within." This yearning is but a pale reflection of how God the Father yearns over His children. Our Father's whole work in our lives moves toward forming Christ and His love within, thus bearing the Spirit's "fruit." The writer of Hebrews calls it the "peaceable fruit of righteousness" (Heb. 12:11). God sees us as positionally righteous in Christ, but He also makes us increasingly righteous and loving day by day. Loving Christians permit God to nurture them in the Lord; that is, the Holy Spirit "forming Christ within." Real believers thus become like their Lord, and they bear the same fruit He did.

Often one hears it said that the "fruit" of a Christian is another Christian. This is not exactly true! Christians of course must witness and win others to faith in their Lord. But that emerges out of Spirit-directed sacrificial *service*. The fruit of the Spirit—the quality of fruit that Christ epitomized in His character—centers in Spirit-directed, sanctified living and loving. Paul pleaded the principle in the Galatians passage quoted above (Gal. 4:19). Paul urged God's people in Galatia to grow up in Christ and permit the Holy Spirit to develop Christlike love and holiness in their lives. And that results in the fruit that the Holy Spirit produces. These words explain why Paul so wanted the Galatians to understand what the true fruit of the Spirit means in the believer's life (Gal. 5:22-23). Love lies at its core.

It is most intriguing when one compares the qualities of

agape in the love chapter (1 Cor. 13) to Paul's list of "the fruit of the Spirit" in Galatians 5:22-23. The parallelism is striking (see fig. 4.1).

1 Corinthians 13	Galatians 5:22–23
Patience	Patience
Kindness	Kindness
Not Jealous	Joy
Not Arrogant	Gentleness
Not Counting Evil	Self-Control
Not Provoked	Peace
Holy	Goodness
Selfless	
Enduring	Faithfulness
Humble	

Figure 4.1

This parallelism provides a penetrating explanation as to why a Bible scholar once said that Paul's passage in Galatians 5:22-23 should be punctuated with the word *love* in verse 22 followed by a colon, not a comma as many versions have it. Thus it would read, "The fruit of the Spirit is love: joy, peace, and so forth"; *not* "The fruit of the Spirit is love, joy, and so forth." This implies that the fruit of the Spirit is primarily love, out of which flows the other graces of joy, peace, and so forth. No punctuation occurs in the original Greek passage, so it can be legitimately punctuated in English as the context requires. Thus in light of the incredible similarity between the two passages in Galatians and 1 Corinthians, the fruit of the Spirit is clearly *love* (*agape*) defined in detail in 1 Corinthians 13 as well as Galatians 5:22-23. Out of love flows all the Christian attributes and virtues that Paul mentions in the two passages. So, the agape love life becomes the full-orbed fruitful life, all wrought by the indwelling Holy Spirit.

Now an in-depth look at each aspect of the fruit of love should prove helpful in the Spirit's work of developing a fruitful life. Henry Drummond presented many insightful thoughts on this aspect of the love chapter. Recall how he called the various aspects of agape love the spectrum of love; then went on to ask:

> Will you observe what its elements are? Will you notice that they have common names; that they are virtues that we hear about every day; that they are things that can be practised by every man in every place in life; and how, by a multitude of small things and ordinary virtues, the supreme thing, the *summum bonum,* is made up? (See p. 34).

Here are a few more thoughts and admonitions to add to Drummond's spectrum.

Joy

Christian joy becomes a beautiful blossom that sends forth its lovely fragrance in the believer's life. The prophet Nehemiah said, "The joy of the LORD is your strength" (Neh. 8:10). Nothing appears quite so contagious or winsomely attractive to the world as Christian joy. Notice that the prophet calls it the joy of the Lord. Jesus termed it "My joy" (John 17:13). It therefore cannot be an earthly, temporal joy. God's people filled with love are not happy simply because circumstances seem pleasant or because they have become positive-thinking people. Love suffers long in adversity. As circumstances seem to conspire to rob a believer of his or her joy, the Spirit steps in and creates endurance and faithfulness. And even though life may be in turmoil, joy resides within, for it is the joy of the Lord, and nothing can destroy that. Abiding in Christ and drawing on His life-giving strength guarantees His joy welling up regardless of life's difficulties because the Holy Spirit creates God's "love-joy" fruit.

Of course believers do not always "bubble over." Yet we can have "joy unspeakable and full of glory" (1 Peter 1:8 KJV). Mere emotion does not constitute the true joy of the Lord. Rather, real joy emerges as a satisfying inner knowledge that God remains faithful and strong to meet any trial regardless of what life hurls across one's path (Rom. 8:28). In that knowledge and assurance a fruit-bearing Christian rejoices.

Peace

Faithfully abiding in the Vine and drawing on God's strength will produce love-fruit that the Bible calls "peace." Paul described it as "the peace of God, which passeth all understanding" (Phil. 4:7 KJV). Again, as in the case of joy, Jesus called it "My peace" (John 14:27). As one commentator says, "When Jesus says, 'Peace,' he actually gives what the word says. It is not a lovely-looking package that is empty inside, but one that is filled with the heavenly reality far more beautiful than the covering in which it is wrapped."[1] Only the Holy Spirit can create that quality of peace. Priceless, yet strangely elusive, multitudes clamor after this beautiful experience. The fact that volumes on how to obtain inner peace line the shelves of bookstores verifies it. Everyone appears to be on an unbridled quest for that mysterious something called "peace of mind." People gather by the thousands for interviews with psychiatrists, hoping to find peace for their troubled lives. Conferences abound on the subject. Others try every avenue imaginable in search of this blessing. They make all the eros scenes that human ingenuity can conjure up: pleasure, wealth, position, drugs, sex, crime, or whatever. As F. B. Meyer said, "Our natures sigh for rest, as an ocean shell, when placed to the ear, seems to cry for the untroubled depths of its native home." People in their eros deception turn everywhere, it seems, except to the *one* source where true peace can be found, in our Lord Jesus Christ. His promise remains true: "Peace I leave with you; My peace I give to you; not as the world gives do I give to you. Let not your heart be troubled, nor let it be fearful" (John 14:27). And the basis of this wonderful promise, as we find in 1 John 4:18, reads, "There is no fear in love; but perfect love casts out fear, because fear involves punishment, and the one who fears is not perfected in love."

Let it again be noticed, it is *His* peace. One does not strive for it. Nor will work produce it. Christ generously generates it in those who faithfully follow Him. Oceanographers tell us that below the surface of the world's great oceans, a layer of calm, still water rests. All remains quiet except the gentle flow of the deep ocean currents. They call it "the cushion of the sea." On the surface of the waters, winds and storms whip the sea into a fury. But below, in the cushion, all is calm—so the fruit-bearing Christian life. Surface circumstances may blow up a serious storm. When one gets caught in the frenzy, life seems anything but pleasant. Yet, believers who abide in the Vine bear the peaceable fruit of faith's rest. They move through the turbulent sea in the cushion, deeply abiding in Christ. The surface may be in a turmoil, yet deep within, the calm of the Spirit rules as the currents of His leadership move one along in the will of God. A serenity of heart prevails because of the consciousness that "our times are in the hands of God." That is peace.

Make no mistake; realism must not be rejected in the quest for the peace of God. Fruit-bearing believers do not deny life's difficulties. Remember, God's agape love is a tough love that forces us to face reality. Still, believers possess true victory and deep satisfaction in the midst of life's situations. Thus, the maturing, loving Christian can have a tear in the eye and peace in the heart at the same time. Only fruit-bearing believers in the Lord Jesus can understand that mystery and experience it.

Patience

Another fruit that bursts out on the branches of those who love Christ with all their hearts Paul calls *patience*. One writer has defined this term as the "strength to defer anger, and the contentedness to bear injuries." Clearly this word depicts a quality of patience in regard to *people*. Chrysostom, the great preacher of Constantinople, said that patience describes the quality of grace that God gives to the Christian who could in justice seek revenge, but refuses to do so. The fruit can constantly be seen in the life of our Lord Jesus Christ. His attitude toward the people He encountered always displayed such a quality. How exasperating it must have been at times when even the twelve apostles missed everything He tried to teach them. Then look at the example of Peter's denying the Lord three times. Yet, Jesus never rejected them in impatience. He truly epitomized longsuffering. If we would bear the kind of fruit that flows from Christ's example, the fruit of patience must characterize all interpersonal relationships.

Kindness

Kindness makes up another cluster of beautiful love-fruit that Christian branches bear. This word is akin to *goodness*, and at times the Bible translators interpret it that way. It implies a particular sort of goodness that displays deep sensitivity to others. One definition expresses it as a sweetness that moves us to be gracious and courteous and easy to be reconciled when we have been wronged. This particular word appears only in the New Testament. It cannot be found in secular Greek. But this is exactly what the secular world sorely needs to see in believers. Only the fruit-bearing Christian can display it in any genuine reality and thus challenge the secular scene.

Goodness

The fruit of goodness takes its rightful place on the believer's branch. This word appears often in the Scriptures. An interesting incident that illustrates its meaning occurred during our Lord's earthly ministry. A man came to Him and asked, "Teacher, what good deed shall I do that I may obtain eternal life?" Jesus retorted, "Why are you asking Me about what is good? There is only One who is good" (Matt. 19:16-17). The man asked a common question. The anomaly of our nature is that even though we are sinful, most of us are concerned about doing and being good. Jesus put the record straight. There can be only One who is ultimately good: God. In Himself He forms the basis of all true goodness. So doing good and being good means to be Godlike.

On a mere human level, of course, God's infinite quality of goodness can never be attained. To be good in this profound sense lies far beyond human achievement. Yet in Christ we are by faith declared good; but more, by God's superabundant grace, we actually bear in our lives the fruit of God's goodness as we walk in the Spirit's fullness and love.

Experiencing God's grace of goodness should not be understood as becoming a do-gooder. Rather, it denotes a strong goodness that the Spirit alone inspires. It centers in being counted righteous by God and doing righteous deeds by faith in Christ. It means, as one commentator expressed it, "Living virtuously and equipped at every point." A genuine Spirit-empowered attempt to be helpful to others in every phase of life constitutes its essence. "So then, while we have opportunity, let us do good to all men, and especially to those who are of the household of faith" (Gal. 6:10). That creates Christlikeness in the highest sense. As the believer abides in the true Vine and bears the Spirit's fruit, he or she can do just that.

Faithfulness

Faithfulness is another fruit of the Spirit that displays a manifestation of God's love. This term is the common word for "trustworthiness." It denotes a person who is totally reliable, just as God can be trusted as reliable in all things. Honesty and justice and fidelity in what one professes and promises permeates the principle. This fruit bears an active role; it grows out of love and vibrant faith in God. Obviously, faithfulness to Christ will make one trustworthy to others.

Gentleness

With faithfulness as a basic stance before God, a proper attitude and relationship to people becomes another lovely fruit of the Spirit; the Bible calls it "gentleness." This fruit of love shines forth the glory of the Vine, Jesus Christ, for He was such a man. Jesus said, "I am gentle and humble in heart" (Matt. 11:29). He further stated, "Blessed are the gentle, for they shall inherit the earth" (Matt. 5:5). This grace requires a threefold understanding. In the first place, it signifies a submission to the will of God (Matt. 11:29). It further means that a gentle Christian is teachable, one not too proud to learn. Finally, it exalts the spirit and attitude of consideration (1 Cor. 4:21). The adjectival form of the word refers to an animal that has been trained and brought under control. For the fruit-bearing Christian, it signifies that when one feels wronged, no display of resentment or vengeance arises. The exact opposites of gentleness are arrogance, vehemence, bitterness, wildness, revenge, and violence. Of course our Lord never exhibited any of these attitudes. And we must make no mistake, meekness cannot be equated with weakness; Jesus was anything but a weak man. Gentleness and meekness make for strength.

Self-Control

The final fruit that blossoms because of the constant work of the Holy Spirit can best be termed "self-control." Ancient philosophers used this word to convey the concept of self-mastery. It applies to the person who has mastered all of his or her desires and love of sensual pleasure. Eros becomes dethroned. Paul employed the term in relationship to an athlete's discipline of his body (1 Cor. 9:25) and to the Christian's mastery of sex (1 Cor. 7:9). Strength of character resides at the heart of the idea. Thus it becomes possible for Christians to so master themselves that they find themselves able to be the right kind of self-giving servants to others.

All this creates the picture of a fruit-bearing branch filled with the love of Christ. The concept obviously relates to every area of life. It touches all interpersonal relationships, especially in the home and family. Paul made that very clear in Ephesians 5:22-6:9. These implications would make a book in themselves, but everything can be summarized by saying, Agape love gives birth to a beautiful life.

It still seems an almost unbelievable order. Nonetheless, the demand confronts every believer. How can one produce such a beautiful cluster of fruit? We have already seen the primary principle in answer to that foundational question: God's love comes by the filling work of the Spirit bearing His fruit within. But how do we see it actually effected in daily life? What makes up our responsibility in fruit-bearing?

The Basis of Fruit Bearing

Our Lord laid down the basic dynamics of bearing His fruit when He said:

> I am the true vine, and My Father is the vinedresser. Every branch in Me that does not bear fruit, He takes away; and every branch that bears fruit, He prunes it, that it may bear more fruit. You are already clean because of the word which I have spoken to you. Abide in Me, and I in you. As the branch cannot bear fruit of itself, unless it abides in the vine, so neither can you, unless you abide in Me. I am the vine, you are the branches; he who abides in Me, and I in him, he bears much fruit; for apart from Me you can do nothing.

If anyone does not abide in Me, he is thrown away as a branch, and dries up; and they gather them, and cast them into the fire, and they are burned. If you abide in Me, and My words abide in you, ask whatever you wish, and it shall be done for you. By this is My Father glorified, that you bear much fruit, and so prove to be My disciples (John 15:1-8).

Obviously, fruit bearing becomes the essential, responsible task before us.

Jesus' words incorporate several important principles. First we ask, how does a typical branch, say of a grapevine, bear fruit? By struggling to do so? Of course not! It simply abides in the vine. When it does, the life-giving sap flows into it. The branch quite naturally bears grapes because of its proper attachment to the vine. It lives off the vine's life-giving sustenance. That makes up its basic design. Therefore, when we as branches abide in the Vine, Jesus Christ, His own life-giving power in the person of the Holy Spirit flows into us in fullness, and we naturally bear fruit. We have already seen this idea in principle; now we must examine it in depth.

Let it be understood once more: No mere humanistic struggle results in bearing the Spirit's fruit; it occurs because the Holy Spirit resides within and His power flows in and through us. In the final analysis, love is His fruit, not ours. A struggle ensues to be sure, but it is not a battle to bear fruit by human determination. The effort centers in permitting Christ's life to be formed within and then lived out in the power of the Spirit. The struggle is of *faith*, not the Law. Thus, we are back to the basic ideas of surrender and faith in the Christian experience. May we always be conscious of the fact that faith and love go hand in hand. But again, let it be stressed, fruit-bearing does entail discipline. The believer is anything but passive in the process, although the life and power come from our Lord. And what is that goal of faith's battle to bear the fruit of love? *Abiding in Christ!* To this end we diligently work. Abiding in our Lord is the clue to discovering a fruitful life of love, just as Jesus said. This principle now raises the very practical question concerning the nature of our part in abiding in Christ so we can bear fruit of the Spirit and remain in His fullness. What are the spiritual disciplines we must practice to stay in a dynamic fellowship with Jesus Christ?

Abiding in Christ

Our Lord spoke specifically and pointedly when He laid out the absolute necessity of abiding in Him if we aspire to experience genuine spirituality and love in our lives. Recall His word: "Abide in Me, and I in you. As the branch cannot bear fruit of itself, unless it abides in the vine, so neither can you, unless you abide in Me" (John 15:4). Expressed simply: no abiding means no fruit.

Some practical issues surface out of this admonition of our Lord. First, notice the progression that Jesus uses concerning fruit in the full passage—John 15:1-8—quoted above. He speaks of fruit, more fruit, and finally much fruit, or we can say, much love. The much fruit displays the Father's plan for us all. Not only does this glorify the Father, it demonstrates to the world that we are Christ's disciples (John 15:8). Secondly, as already discovered, the passage makes it abundantly clear that the fruit is an attribute of God. We embody *His* love. Our Lord reminded us, "Without Me you can do nothing." So we must pay the price to abide in Jesus if we aspire to bear much fruit. We have to work at it. Paul wrote to young Timothy, admonishing him to exercise "love and . . . self-discipline" (2 Tim. 1:7). Our discipline parallels our loving. And do not forget, as Henry Drummond pointed out, "No man can become a saint in his sleep; and to fulfil the condition required demands a certain amount of prayer and meditation and time, just as improvement in any direction, bodily or mental, requires preparation and care" (p. 49).

Four basic disciplines lay the foundation for abiding in our Lord, and each one demands a real spiritual effort: (1) keeping our sins constantly confessed becomes an important exercise; (2) we must regularly be found in God's Word; (3) a life of prayer is inescapable; (4) witnessing to our faith assumes a central role. It will be good to look at each one of these areas. Henry Drummond would resonate with each one.

Confession of Sin in Abiding in Christ

Good growth in grace and much fruit do not come without the discipline of dealing with specific sins as they relate to one's personal life and relationships. We have touched on this idea when we discussed seeking the Spirit's fullness. Now we need to see it in some detail. The reason for doing so is clear: One simply cannot abide in Christ and harbor known, conscious sins at the same time. Remember, no fullness means no fruit. This discipline constitutes the pruning process that our Lord spoke of. For example, the great Shantung revival of 1927-36 in North China broke out only when the missionaries began to pray and face God concerning their specific, individual sins. Not until then did the true power of the Spirit came upon them. It produced a fascinating story.

The account begins in the Chinese seaport of Chefoo. Because of a volatile political situation in North China, many of the missionary personnel of Shantung Province gathered as a group in the seaport city until the unrest ceased. Bertha Smith, one of those dedicated missionaries, tells the story:

> One of our number, Mrs. Charles Culpepper, Sr., had suffered much from optical neuritis, which had left only partial vision in the eye affected. A few months before we were called to Chefoo, the good eye began to cause trouble. The mission doctor in Laichowfu advised her to go to Peking for treatment.

The Culpepper family went to Union Medical College Hospital. Due to the philanthropy of John D. Rockefeller, Jr., the world's best specialists were to be found there. The eye specialist at that time was from Vienna, Austria. He changed her glasses but gave no encouragement about an improvement in the general condition of her eyes.

During those days in Chefoo when we often had fellowship . . . and heard . . . how God had marvelously healed all sorts of diseases, Mrs. Culpepper started having eye trouble again. There was still no eye specialist nearer than Peking, which was over 200 miles away. She did not believe he could do much for her, even if she could receive his care. She truly felt discouraged.

One evening the thought came to her to ask . . . the prayer group to pray that the Lord would heal her. It was a very difficult thing to bring herself to do, for she still had the prejudice which had been in her mind for years concerning faith healing. . . .

By that time some of the refugeeing missionaries had returned to the United States, leaving eighteen of us. Some of them said that miracles of bodily healing were granted to first-century Christians as a proof that Jesus had risen from the dead. Now that the New Testament was completed, God expects people to believe the written record. Others said, "My God shall supply every need of yours." Certainly this was a definite need with no human remedy.

Since praying for the sick to be divinely healed had never been in her way of belief or practice, Mrs. Culpepper had never studied the Bible from this viewpoint. It was really the work of the Spirit during those days that brought her life before her like a movie. She began to see her real self as God saw her. Only the power of the Holy Spirit could have given her strength to talk very frankly with her husband, confessing sins against him and others. Even greater courage was given her to say to the whole group that she was most unworthy to be one of their number.

She was not the only one who was getting altogether right with God during that week. All of us who expected to pray for the eye were doing deep heart-searching. We were calling upon the Holy Spirit, who is Light, to shine into the deep recesses of our beings, to reveal anything that he was ready to prune out at that stage of our Christian development.

When the day agreed on arrived, twelve were present in the prayer meeting. Dr. Culpepper read from the fifth chapter of James: "Therefore confess your sins to one another, and pray for one another, that you may be healed. The prayer of a righteous man has great power in its effects" (James 5:16). He did not try to explain it; he was not leaving out anything of which the Bible spoke. He then put some olive oil on Mrs. Culpepper's head and asked all to come up and lay their hands on her head and pray.

I had gone into that room, so far as I knew, absolutely right with the Lord. I would not have dared to go otherwise. But when I stretched my hand out to Mrs. Culpepper's head, I had to bring it back. There stood facing me a missionary with whom there had been a little trouble. In her early years she had been head of a girls' school, but for several years she had been teaching illiterate women to read.

I had been asked to serve as principal in our boys' school in Chefoo while the missionary principal was on furlough. I had majored in education, and by that time had had ten years' experience in teaching and thought that I was "the last word" in education! I had recommended Miss Hartwell to lead daily worship in that school. After a few weeks, I asked another missionary to tell her that methods for teaching old women were not appropriate for high school boys. She was hurt, of course.

But what about my proud self? I did not have a particle of sympathy for her. Right there before everyone, I had to say, Miss Hartwell, I did not have the proper attitude toward you about that school affair. I beg you to forgive me! My hand then joined the others and we prayed.

Had I refused to confess that sin, and joined in the prayer with it covered, I believe that I would have hindered the prayer of the others, and the eye could not have been healed.

Because all were right with God and of one heart, heaven came down! We did not have to wait to see whether or not Mrs. Culpepper's eye was healed! We knew in our hearts that she would never have another attack. The Lord had heard the prayers of such human frailty and had performed a miracle in healing one whom we so loved! She did not put her glasses back on.[2]

The Bible makes it very clear; if we wish to see God's best blessings we must *confess our sins*. John forthrightly states, "If we confess our sins, He is faithful and righteous to forgive us our sins and to cleanse us from all unrighteousness" (1 John 1:9). What are the implications when John urges us to bring our sins to God in confession?

The Meaning of Confession of Sins

At the very outset, look at the intriguing word *confess*. In the language of the New Testament, it is a compound word. John wedded two different words, and the union gave birth to a new, rich truth. The term is comprised of the verb *to say* with a prefix meaning *the same*. Thus, the word that we translate "confess" in our English Bibles literally means "to say the same thing as" or "to assent to" or "to agree with." Confession means that we "agree with" concerning our sins.

With whom, however, do we agree concerning our errors?

The answer is obvious: the Holy Spirit (John 16:7-11). The Spirit of God is the One who puts His convicting finger on specific sins that have warped our walk with Jesus Christ. Therefore, for Christians to confess sins scripturally means "to concede to" or "to agree with" the convicting Spirit of God that some *particular* act of rebellion *truly is a sin*. It implies getting out of one's own self and standing by the Holy Spirit, being objective about the issue, and agreeing with Him as He convicts us of some issue in our lives that is displeasing to God. We take an objective stand with God against our individual sins and acts of rebellion. We agree with God and stop our humanistic rationalizing and excuse making.

This approach casts a doubtful question on general, nonspecific confession of sins. For example, how often we simply pray, "Lord, forgive me of all my sins!"—and that's it. This misses the manner in which the Bible says a Christian should confess sins. Perhaps that accounts for the fact that often no assurance of forgiveness follows our confession. Such an approach to confession of sins may be fitting for a worship service or in a group, but in individual private prayer, this will never do. To confess sins, according to John, means naming them individually, agreeing with the Spirit of God that the particular act of which He convicts truly is a sin. No one sins in an indefinable way; thus, the confession of sin should not be done in an indefinable manner either. They should be confessed one by one and named for what they are. We committed them one by one; they should be confessed in that way. That demands honesty and objectivity, as Bertha Smith discovered. This necessitates lingering before God long enough to permit the Holy Spirit to search one out and place His finger of conviction on those particular deeds that constitute evil. And when the Holy Spirit speaks, we listen. Paul warned us, "Do not grieve the Holy Spirit of God, by whom you were sealed for the day of redemption" (Eph. 4:30).

Furthermore, as implied in the previous chapter, we all have "secret" sins; that is, sins of which we are not aware at our present stage of sanctification and maturity. This should be acknowledged and confessed to our forgiving Father. David prayed, "Who can discern his errors? Acquit me of hidden faults" (Ps. 19:12).

Of course we must forsake our sins in the context of confession. Forsaking sins is presupposed in the biblical concept of confession. But having acknowledged every individual sin before God to which He draws our attention, the assurance comes that the blood of Jesus Christ thoroughly and completely cleanses. The forgiveness of God becomes a marvelous experience indeed. God has committed Himself (1 John 1:9). If we confess our sins, He is *faithful,* faithful to His promise and His attribute of love; and just— Christ bore all the penalty of our sins—to forgive us of our rebellion and cleanse us from *all unrighteousness.* "To forgive" in John's terminology means to wipe out a debt. "To be cleansed" implies the blotting out of a stain. God will not only eradicate all debts, He will even blot out the stain of the memory that may drag one down into spiritual depression and guilt. The Bible says, "As far as the east is from the west, so far has He removed our transgressions from us" (Ps. 103:12). God forgives and remembers your sins no more (Isa. 43:25). If God forgets, so can we, and that is liberty in our souls.

Other Implications

A secondary problem emerges here, however. What if some sins involve relationships with others as well as one's fellowship with God? In such an instance, merely to confess them to God alone proves insufficient to experience the full liberty of Christ's forgiveness. We should confess them to God, of course, but as seen in the previous chapter on the Spirit's fullness, Jesus said we must confess sins to those we offend (Matt. 5:23-24). We cannot avoid the simple truth declared by our Lord Jesus Christ:

If we sin against another person and fellowship becomes strained, restitution must be made to the offended person as well as to God. If we fail to acknowledge our sin and seek forgiveness from those individuals we sin against (as much as is possible in the present circumstances and as God leads), then we cannot expect deep fellowship with God or with one another. Actually, agape love demands that we be right both with God and others. That can be a difficult discipline to follow, but we should remember that love is worth any hardship. If we would but obey Jesus' word on this issue, it would revolutionize our homes, our churches, our nation, and our world. Love can do that. And we should never forget, we must likewise forgive those who sin against us. The Ephesians were urged, "Be kind to one another, tender-hearted, forgiving each other, just as God in Christ also has forgiven you" (Eph. 4:32). Our Lord even went so far as to say, "For if you forgive men for their transgressions, your heavenly Father will also forgive you. But if you do not forgive men, then your Father will not forgive your transgressions" (Matt. 6:14-15). Self-giving love must pervade the entire arena of forgiveness.

Finally, there can even be times when sin manifests itself not simply against God alone or against another single individual. It may be open, known to others, and has brought reproach on the church and our Christian testimony. Does the Bible say anything on this score? James tells us, "Therefore confess your sins to one another, and pray for one another, so that you may be healed" (James 5:16). Does James mean to say that situations arise that necessitate honestly and openly confessing sins to a group or even the entire church? Such seems to be his meaning. This can be difficult, yet, there should be that person or group in the fellowship of believers with whom we can be quite open, honest, and candid about ourselves. The church should always be such a fellowship of love and acceptance.

Care must be taken, however, that this openness never

degenerate into an airing of all our "dirty linen" before the whole world. Some have fallen into this satanic trap. Such an exercise can become very damaging to spiritual health and fellowship. There are some areas of our lives that only God should ever know. Yet at the same time, as a sensitivity to the Holy Spirit grows in the fellowship of the believers, He will grant wisdom so that it will be clear what should be shared and with whom (James 1:5). The basic biblical principle revolves around the reality that sin should be confessed and restitution made in the area or confines of the offense. We simply need to get right with whomever we have sinned against—God, others, or the church. That may in certain cases involve some sort of restitution, the case of Zacchaeus being an example of that truth (Luke 19:1-10).

The blood of Christ is powerful and precious beyond words. What a liberating experience it is when one comes before God in honest confession. A new fellowship with God suddenly bursts into one's experience and life glows. Love comes alive because we abide in our lovely Lord.

Our Lord Jesus Christ urged us to remain in His love (John 15:9). Therefore, the next important exercise we must give ourselves to practice is Bible study.

Bible Study

The Word of God becomes the food for our spirit. We must eat often. Maintaining a healthy diet necessitates keeping some basic truths constantly in mind. We must appreciate the nature of the Bible. We call it the Word of God, and correctly so. The Scriptures themselves declare their divine inspiration. The apostle Peter wrote, "But know this first of all, that no prophecy of Scripture is a matter of one's own interpretation, for no prophecy was ever made by an act of human will, but men moved by the Holy Spirit spoke from God" (2 Peter 1:20-21). Paul likewise held a similar view when he said, "All Scripture is inspired by God and profitable for teaching, for reproof, for correction, for training in righteousness" (2 Tim. 3:16). There can be no mistake in light of what the Bible claims for itself: every page speaks of divine inspiration and thus its truthfulness, profitability, and authority. To realize that God has actually given us this treasure is really marvelous.

If the Bible is God's own Word, it must be cherished and obeyed. Jesus said that he who "keeps," or "guards" His commandments, remains in His love (John 15:10). The word *keeps* or *guards* literally means "watchful care," "to cherish," "to hold as a treasure." This makes it mandatory that we hold to, love, obey, and seek God through His truth. And that implies our commitment to study the Bible. Simply put, there must be a regular disciplined time for study. To snatch just a few verses here and there will never keep us close to abiding in Christ. We should have a definite disciplined study time that we set aside to let God speak to us through the Scriptures. It takes disciplined work and dedication, but there is no escape if we would abide in our Lord. The Word of God becomes the foundation on which we build our lives in the practical understanding of accomplishing the will of God.

The Necessity of Prayer

Not only does Bible study hold a strong priority, disciplined prayer assumes a vital role in abiding in Christ. Probably the most neglected aspect of our Christian experience can be found in the realm of prayer. That can be tragic, because where prayer abounds, God's presence and power abound. To neglect prayer means to neglect God. Samuel Chadwick had it right when he said:

> There is no power like that of prevailing prayer—of Abraham pleading for Sodom, Jacob wrestling in the stillness of the night, Moses standing in the breach, Hannah

intoxicated with sorrow, David heartbroken with remorse and grief, Jesus in sweat of blood. Add to this list from the records of the church your personal observation and experience, and always there is the cost of passion unto blood. Such prayer prevails. It turns ordinary mortals into men of power. It brings power. It brings fire. It brings rain. It brings life. It brings God.

Matthew Henry declared, "When God is ready to pour out unusual mercies, He sets His people a-praying." How are we to engage in that kind and quality of prayer? What constitutes the primary principles of prevailing prayer? They need to be learned.

Praying Correctly

Prayer must be exercised according to the rules if we aspire to abide in Christ and bear fruit. The Bible tells us what makes up these rules. Moreover, the Holy Spirit will guide one into these realities. He has been called the teacher in the school of prayer. And rightly so, for He deeply desires to instruct God's people in effectual prayer (Rom. 8:26).

We should be clear when we speak about the rules of prayer. It by no means implies that prayer is an inflexible, legalistic, wooden framework in which we cram our spiritual exercises. Of all the experiences in the Christian life where real liberty can be found, it can be discovered in prayer. In the final analysis, prayer simply means conversing with God; that is, a divine-human dialogue. Real prayer just invites Jesus into one's life to meet needs. To liken the Holy Spirit to a teacher in the art of prayer is never meant to picture Him as a stern school principal ready to apply the rod if ever in the course of any prayer experience one does not pray exactly according to plan. "Where the Spirit of the Lord is, there is liberty" (2 Cor. 3:17). The Father is amazingly understanding. He looks down into the very heart of our being, and when He finds sincerity and genuine longing,

He smiles. Therefore, one must never get so preoccupied with the forms and patterns of prayer that a childlike look of faith to a loving Father and a pouring out of the deepest desires of the heart somehow get missed.

At the same time, however, a few guidelines should be followed. They will make our intercession purposeful and in line with what the Holy Spirit attempts to teach us as He guides us into a richer and deeper prayer life. Therefore, initially look at the principle of *praying constantly*.

Praying Without Ceasing

Paul urged all believers to "Pray without ceasing" (1 Thess. 5:17). Let's imagine a dialogue with Paul. "What do you mean by this challenge, Paul?" He answers, "First of all, God expects us to have a regular, consistent, disciplined, dedicated prayer life. All have daily needs. Therefore, a prayer time should become a daily spiritual habit, as God wills and permits." We ask, "Paul, must we have a specific time and never ever miss?" He answers, "That's not the primary point nor is some particular posture of the body either! We must not be legalists, just disciplined. A Christian can pray at any hour or in any physical position as long as sincerity and humility arise as foremost in seeking God's Presence. The fact that one gives regular time for prayer and then sincerely intercedes on a consistent basis make up the essentials." "All right," we answer. We must exercise ourselves and be consistent "in season and out of season."

Another implication of Paul's statement to the Thessalonian church can be seen in a home in which hung a plaque that read, "Divine services are conducted here daily." That is sublime. We can pray in all our daily pursuits, whether washing the dishes, working on the job, or merely walking down the street. The Lord Jesus Christ *always* has His ear open to our cry. We need not go through some series of religious exercises to bring our needs and desires to God. Moment by moment we can lift our hearts to His very throne (Heb. 4:16). We should be in a constant attitude of prayer. We can shoot one arrow up to heaven as well as a heavy barrage. Such a privilege becomes a rich source of blessings to the person who will constantly pray. We should live in a spirit of prayer so that at any moment we can call on our gracious heavenly Father and be assured He will hear. Paul said a lot in the little three-word phrase, "Pray without ceasing." "Yes," Paul might answer, "prevailing prayer starts right there." But there is more.

Pray Specifically

A further principle of effective praying centers in the problem that prayer so often is made in such nebulous terms that nothing is actually requested. Simply asking God to bless someone or something in a general way can well miss asking for the actual things needed. The Bible urges us to get to *real issues*. And it applies to ourselves as well as others. If you need wisdom to make a decision, ask God for that specifically. If you need to be drawn closer to Christ, ask for that. If you need to confess sins, name them. Spiritual prayer principles do not exclude physical needs either. If you need a new coat, ask for a new coat. Christians who pray in this manner find that in seeking specific things, far more answers to prayer are forthcoming.

Quite naturally, this principle applies to praise as well. We should praise, bless, and thank the Lord for all His goodness. And we should name His blessings. The old admonition to "count our many blessings, name them one by one" hits the target dead center. God deserves our praise and gratitude.

Praying in God's Will

When Jesus agonized in the garden of Gethsemane, He ended His earnest petition with the phrase, "Yet it must not be what I want, but what you want" (Matt. 26:39 PHILLIPS). We too must ask for things that reside *in the will of God.* Only then can we expect God to answer. John tells us that "We can approach God with confidence for this reason: if we make requests which accord with his will he listens to us" (1 John 5:14 NEB). Effectual prayer is born when that prayer ascends to God according to His will and purpose.

The question therefore becomes: How can one know the will of God in prayer? First, reading the Bible stands as absolutely essential. When prayer requests emerge in keeping with the Scriptures, one knows that the petition coincides with God's will. The Bible abounds with examples of how God longs to answer prayer made according to His will.

Moreover, Paul has told us: "And in the same way the Spirit also helps our weakness; for we do not know how to pray as we should, but the Spirit Himself intercedes for us with groanings too deep for words; and He who searches the hearts knows what the mind of the Spirit is, because He intercedes for the saints according to the will of God" (Rom. 8:26-27). As we quiet ourselves before God, the Holy Spirit will speak and show us what to pray for. His inner witness is vital because the Bible does not deal with many specifics in our contemporary life; in many instances the Scriptures lay out the general principles. Therefore, real prayer can never be a mere monologue. The Holy Spirit wishes to speak to us in prayer and reveal that which is in keeping with the mind of our heavenly Father. Of course, we may not always know for absolute certainty; therefore, we should always conclude our prayer by sincerely saying, "Yet not My will, but Thine be done" (Luke 22:42). Jesus did.

Praying in Faith

Another word must be considered right here. To end prayer with the phrase "not My will, but Thine be done" must never be used as an excuse for failing to pray what the Bible calls "the prayer of faith." The Scriptures speak very emphatically about that. The epistle of James states, "But let him ask in faith without any doubting, for the one who doubts is like the surf of the sea driven and tossed by the wind. For let not that man expect that he will receive anything from the Lord" (James 1:6-7). God puts a high premium on faith as one prays. Our Lord went so far as to say, "If you have faith as a mustard seed, you shall say to this mountain, 'Move from here to there,' and it shall move; and nothing shall be impossible to you" (Matt. 17:20). Prayer can move mountains—mountains of problems and difficulties can be uprooted by honest, faithful prayer.

Such faith does not come easy. But remember the Bible disciplines. Faith comes through meditating on the scriptural promises that relate to prayer, understanding the character of Christ, becoming convinced that the things one asks for are in keeping with God's will, and remembering that our Lord will keep His promises. Bible meditation and praying in faith are inseparable. Moreover, the Holy Spirit inspires faith to claim God's promises regarding prayer as we pray in His will and rest on His Word.

We must be careful not to put faith in prayer itself. The heavenly Father stands as the object of true faith. "Power belongs to God" (Ps. 62:11), not us. Yet we can rely on the Holy Spirit— He will come to our aid and assist us to pray properly in faith if we have our hearts open to His inner work.

Prayer in Jesus' Name

The Savior said, "I say to you, if you shall ask the Father for anything, He will give it to you in My name. Until now you have asked for nothing in My name; ask, and you will receive, that your joy may be made full" (John 16:23-24). These verses emphasize the centrality of praying in Jesus' name. Of course, people often end their prayers with that phrase or something like it. But far more is involved in our Lord's statement than just pinning a pious platitude on the end of our prayers. What does it mean?

The heart of the idea lies in the truth that the entire Christ-event undergirds our asking. We pray in all that Jesus is and all He has accomplished in His life, death, and resurrection. As an astute Bible commentator expressed it:

> In all the connections in which this important phrase occurs
> το ονομα (in my name) . . . denotes the revelation by
> which we know Jesus. . . . This revelation covers his person
> as well as his work. It is concentrated in his titles, of which
> we have many, but it takes in all that makes these titles the
> shining designations that they are. And (in) has its natural
> sense of sphere: "in union with," "in connection with." This
> (in) draws a circle around the action of asking, the
> boundary is the (name). . . . Hence not "on the basis of my
> name," "through my name," which would change the
> preposition. To pray in Jesus' name naturally involves faith
> in the revelation, also that the petition abide in the circle
> of that revelation.[3]

We are sinners. We are unclean. None are righteous, no not one (Rom. 3:10). But Jesus Christ has made access to and acceptance before God possible by His atoning death and resurrection. Through Him and in Him alone believers are declared righteous and thus worthy to stand in the Father's presence. All power belongs to our Lord, so in His name, and all that it implies, we pray and thus are assured we will be heard. In that way alone we can come boldly to the throne of grace, and find help (Heb. 4:16).

To pray in Jesus' name does not mean we must invariably address the Father. We can pray to Jesus, even to the Holy Spirit. The Trinity has an open ear. Yet our prayers, inspired by the Holy Spirit, should be directed *primarily* to the Father in Jesus' name. The so-called model prayer of Jesus makes this clear. He taught us to pray, "Our Father, who art in heaven" (Matt. 6:9).

Thus, when we pray we approach God humbly, not in our own righteousness, strength, or ability, but in the name, power, and righteousness of the total work and person of our Lord and Savior Jesus Christ. Our prayers are acceptable only because of Him and His redemptive work. To realize this truth constitutes the essence of bold prayer. Fervor, zeal, or even sincerity do not make prayers acceptable before a righteous and holy God, even though they have their proper place in prayer. Rather, praying in Jesus' strong name permits the loving Father to hear and answer.

Praying from a Pure Heart

The psalmist tells us, "If I regard wickedness in my heart, the Lord will not hear" (Ps. 66:18). Perhaps the greatest hindrance to answered prayer is unconfessed sins. To harbor consciously some specific sin—or sins—destroys vital fellowship with God. Prayer should, therefore, begin by quieting oneself before the Father, listening to the voice of the Spirit as He points out our sins, and then honestly acknowledge the situation. As the Holy Spirit places His convicting finger on the evil, confessing and forsaking it becomes mandatory. But that principle has been made amply clear to those who would abide in Christ and bear fruit.

The Content of Prayer

The content of our prayers is simple. We should first praise God and honor His holy name. Thanksgiving supplies an essential element of our conversation with our Lord. Then we intercede for others—the lost, believers in their needs, family, friends, government leaders, Christian leaders, and for whoever the Holy Spirit burdens our heart. Of course, we bring before God a host of other situations where divine intervention and aid are needed. Finally, we pray for our own needs, wishes, circumstances, and the like. And never forget to keep sins confessed up to date. As rudimentary as all this may sound, it supplies the content and sets a logical and sequential pattern for prayer. And we must always recall the great promise in James' word: "The effective prayer of a righteous man can accomplish much" (James 5:16).

All that has been said concerning various elements of prayer can be summed up in the phrase, "Praying in the Spirit." Paul states that Christians should "Pray at all times *in the Spirit*" (Eph. 6:18, emphasis added). The Holy Spirit, as the Teacher in the school of prayer, instructs in the rudiments and the sophistications of prayer for effective intercession. He inspires faith and lifts one's very soul into the presence of the Savior as He prays through the Christian (Rom. 8:26). In other words, He alone makes prayer alive and effectual. All dynamic prayer comes through the activity of the blessed Spirit of God. Therefore, to hear His voice as one prays and permit Him to speak through the human heart to the heart of God forms the foundation of prevailing prayer. In this manner, prayer becomes a vital communication with the Father in heaven. What an adventure with the Spirit! S. D. Gordon put it all together when he said:

> The greatest thing anyone can do for God and man is to pray. It is not the only thing. But it is the chief thing. . . . The great people of the earth today are the people who pray. I do not mean those who talk about prayer; nor those who say they believe in prayer; nor yet those who can explain about prayer; but I mean those people who *take* time and pray.

All loving Christians can affirm that. Now one more abiding discipline must be addressed.

Sharing Our Faith

Finally, the principle of sharing our faith becomes a vital ingredient to abiding in Christ and bearing the love-fruit. Christ has called us all to be witnesses (Acts 1:8). We have a wonderful message to tell. How desperately the world needs to hear that message. The Bible calls it "the gospel," the Good News of our Lord Jesus Christ, which Paul calls the "power of God for salvation" (Rom. 1:16). That makes up our word of witness, and God expects us to share it as He regularly opens doors of opportunity. We shall have much more to say about this discipline of witness in the last chapter of this book.

Conclusion

All of these simple disciplines may seem so elementary that we expect to mature beyond them. Nothing could be further from the truth. As long as we live on earth, we must be right before God, keep in the Word of God, come before the Lord in prayer, and go into the world sharing Jesus Christ. That keeps us abiding in the Lord and in turn permits the Holy Spirit to flow through us and create the fruit of genuine Christian love. The "much fruit" that Jesus spoke of depends on it.

Implied in all of this resides the reality that we must give ourselves to the will of God if we would love as Jesus loved. We remember that our Lord said He came to do God's will and the things that please Him (John 8:29). To love means to follow our Lord's example and be obedient. We turn to that fundamental aspect of the greatest thing in the world.

Endnotes

1. R. C. H. Lenski, *The Interpretation of St. John's Gospel* (Minneapolis: Augsburg, 1963), 1366-67.
2. Bertha Smith, *Go Home and Tell* (Nashville: Broadman Press, 1965), 14-17.
3. Lenski, *St. John's Gospel*, 991.

5 | *Love Obeys*

If you keep My commandments, you will abide in My love.

John 15:10

In the entire realm of bearing the fruit of agape love, we must become vividly aware of one thing—true love for God always elicits true obedience to His will. Jesus made this most clear when He said, "He who has My commandments and keeps them, he it is who loves Me; and he who loves Me shall be loved by My Father, and I will love him, and will disclose Myself to him" (John 14:21). Our Lord went on to state most emphatically, "If anyone loves Me, he will keep My word; and My Father will love him, and We will come to him, and make Our abode with him. He who does not love Me does not keep My words; and the word which you hear is not Mine, but the Father's who sent Me" (John 14:23-24). We dare not miss this issue; if we love God, we obey God. It is that forthright—and that fundamental. Love on the agape plane must always be understood in that context. C. S. Lewis reminds us, "Love in the Christian sense, does not mean an emotion. It is a state not of the feelings, but of the will."¹ God's love, as we have learned, is to be seen as active love—it faces facts. That implies a substance that far supersedes any emotion; and that substance and essence centers in obeying the Lord in all of life. The apostle Paul said:

> I urge you therefore, brethren, by the mercies of God, to present your bodies a living and holy sacrifice, acceptable to God, which is your spiritual service of worship. And do not be conformed to this world, but be transformed by the

renewing of your mind, that you may prove what the will of God is, that which is good and acceptable and perfect (Rom. 12:1-2).

We will never experience the greatest thing in the world until we exercise the greatest thing God demands: undiluted obedience to Christ's lordship in our lives.

The Problem

The Christian ideal of love revolves around sincere surrender of our will to Jesus Christ. Yet we are all aware that so often we disappoint God and become disobedient. In one sense, we may love God and desire with all our heart to do His will but still find ourselves slipping into disobedience, sin, and even at times outright rebellion. The old eros approach can overtake us. Why the paradox? Why, if God commands obedience and we love Him, do we find ourselves missing the mark? The resolution of this dilemma would surely do much to deepen and mature our love for Jesus Christ. We need to find the answer.

The Promise of Victory

Let us be certain at the outset—victory can be achieved in and through our Victor, the Lord Jesus Christ. The Scriptures speak plainly that God produces power over temptation to disobedience as well as grants forgiveness when we do fail. Our Lord's promises of becoming a conqueror abound in the Bible:

But thanks be to God, who always leads us in triumph in Christ, and manifests through us the sweet aroma of the knowledge of Him in every place (2 Cor. 2:14).

For the law of the Spirit of life in Christ Jesus has set you free from the law of sin and of death (Rom. 8:2).

In all these things we are more than conquerors through
Him who loved us (Rom. 8:37 NIV).

Conclusion: In Christ Jesus the battle has been won. He has
conquered. The paradox has been resolved, but we must learn
how to appropriate Christ's victory in our daily lives. Love
requires it.

Still, few Christians seem to experience the overcoming life,
even though the Scriptures promise it. Often we seem to grovel
in the dust of defeat that drains away joy and peace in Christ.
The result: Love wanes. Much fruit degenerates into little fruit.
The mentality among many believers is like the early disciples
between Friday and Sunday during that first Passion Week. Hope
all but dies. Why? The reason usually centers in either a failure
to face up to certain realities about the battle of the spiritual
life or an attempt to achieve victory in a way that gives no promise
of success—or both. These issues need addressing.

The Pressing Problem

A deadly war wages. Paul's words ring true: "Our struggle is
not against flesh and blood, but against the rulers, against the
powers, against the world forces of this darkness, against the
spiritual forces of wickedness in the heavenly places" (Eph.
6:12). Believers are engaged in serious conflict. The mind of
the flesh, incited by Satan and demonic influences, engages the
indwelling Holy Spirit, and the battle rages on (Gal. 5:17). The
resulting warfare can only be described as rugged and rough.
The "old man" in all of us wars to the death against the Spirit,
and vice versa. Jeremiah said, "The heart is more deceitful than
all else and is desperately sick; who can understand it?" (Jer.
17:9). Our Lord Jesus Christ stated, "For from within, out of the
heart of men, proceed the evil thoughts, fornications, thefts,
murders, adulteries" (Mark 7:21). We can climb to the mountain
heights of love and adoration of God, and in a moment find the

old man taking over and plummeting us down to the muck of evil and lust. When we yield to the flesh, or the devil, victory dissipates. It presents a depressing scenario.

The problem compounds itself because we seem so powerless to do anything about it. And right there many Christians make a basic blunder; they fight on and attempt to gain victory along some path that proves to be a perfect dead end. Strive as one may, fighting in human strength alone and with one's own devices to achieve victory assures defeat. What makes up those futile humanistic eros efforts to cope?

False Roads to Victory

The first path that many tread, only to be disillusioned and defeated, is commonly called the *sinless-perfection* route. Some have convinced themselves that they abide in a state of perfect love where they can no longer sin. This error can be dismissed quickly. Neither the Bible nor experience presents any validity to this approach. In this life we will never achieve a state where we no longer sin (1 John 1:8). To think it possible is only to deceive oneself; and worse, to ignore real sin. But we have labored that point sufficiently.

Another erroneous road that carries many a traveler and leads to an impasse can be called the *resignation* route. That is, some give themselves over to a spirit of resignation to the inevitable. They say, "Well, if I cannot live above sin and God will continually forgive me, why get excited or unduly concerned about it? If I am under grace and not works, I will not get up-tight over the situation." But God sees this attitude as deviant from His plan as that of sinless perfection—perhaps even more. This approach has historically been called the heresy of *antinomianism*. We must never forget that sin constitutes a *real issue;* it can seriously damage and disrupt fellowship and our love for God. Paul countered this kind of argument forthrightly in Romans 6:1-2: "What shall we say then? Are we to continue in sin that grace might increase? May it never be!" This detour from God's pathway will never direct us to our desired destination of agape love and victory.

Another route often run can be termed the *suppression syndrome*. Knowing the seriousness of the sin problem, one ardently attempts to defeat evil with human energy, striving to suppress sin by one's own willpower. Many struggle on that stretch of road. We all try this venture at times, especially if we do not know God's way of the overcoming life. Of course, we gain a certain measure of victory and blessing, but those temptations we seem powerless to overcome continually plague us. We pray about it, ask God for strength to overcome, determine never to do it any more, even promise God we will absolutely not fall again. Of course, we usually leave the door open, by praying, "By your grace we won't fall again!" Yet, in the back of our minds, we know we probably will—and usually we do.

No sincere Christian really wants to sin. The Holy Spirit lives in our lives, and we know that sin grieves Him and drains away Christ's peace, power, and the fullness of His love. But evil constantly besieges the citadel of our high resolution until a breach in the wall is made and down in defeat we go once more. So back to God we go with confession and new resolves to do better next time, seeking a fresh infilling of the Spirit—only to repeat the same pattern over and over again. What a depressing cycle!

The despair of it all, the harder we battle down these humanistic roads, the worse it seems to get. We finally get to the point of anguish and cry out with Paul, "Wretched man that I am! Who will set me free from the body of this death?" (Rom. 7:24). At that point of despair, however, hope arises. If God can move us to desperation and bring us to the end of ourselves, He may then be able to reveal *His road* to victory. We may well have to be brought to the place of absolute frustration before realizing that retreating into an unreal world of sinless perfection, resigning oneself to sin's captive claim, or striving to fight the battle in mere human strength leads to ultimate defeat. At that point, if we truly want to be obedient *at any cost*, God opens marvelous truths in the Bible, pointing to the royal road of becoming a conquering, obedient, loving Christian. Let it be repeated: There is victory in Jesus Christ.

The Prime Principle

John formulated the foundational principle of spiritual victory in his first epistle when he wrote: "This is the victory that has overcome the world—our faith" (1 John 5:4). The beloved disciple desperately wanted to show us that *the way of victory is the way of faith*. It holds true for salvation and also for sanctification. This "faith principle"—which we have hinted at several times—points to the true path in becoming a conqueror in Christ. Failing to grasp this essential idea can spell defeat in spiritual battles. In the final analysis, lack of faith forces one into a wilderness of wearisome warfare (Heb. 4:2). Victory comes only through faith: believing God and moving into the "Promised Land" where enemies are conquered. Paul presented the same spiritual plan, stating, "In addition to all, taking up the shield of faith with which you will be able to extinguish all the flaming missiles of the evil one" (Eph. 6:16). Belief forms the basis of all Christian conquest, in godly living as well as in redemption. The hymn writer had it right: "Faith is the victory, we know, that overcomes the world" (John Yates, "Faith Is the Victory").

Dynamic faith must have an object, however. It will not do simply to say, "Have faith!" and all will be well. Such pious statements may sound spiritual and supportive, but they are far too indefinite to possess any positive power. Genuine faith must always find its beginning basis in objective reality—the Truth. Truth as the object or ground of faith must be understood in a twofold sense.

First, believers have the objective, propositional truth of God, the Scriptures. The Bible has a vital role to play as an object of vibrant belief (Rom. 10:17). Second, Christians also confront the truth through the living Truth, Jesus Christ Himself. He always stands as the ultimate goal of our faith endeavors. Therefore, when we say faith has Truth as its object, it should be understood in this twofold manner. The written Word of God leads us to the Living Word of God—Jesus Christ. That is how promises are fulfilled. What, then, constitutes the biblical truth concerning our personal experience of Jesus Christ that forms the foundation to lift our eyes to the Lord so we may experience victory and a life of obedient love? That becomes the key question. Paul answers and declares the following spiritual reality:

What shall we say then? Are we to continue in sin that grace might increase? May it never be! How shall we who died to sin still live in it? Or do you not know that all of us who have been baptized into Christ Jesus have been baptized into His death? Therefore we have been buried with Him through baptism into death, in order that as Christ was raised from the dead through the glory of the Father, so we too might walk in newness of life. For if we have become united with Him in the likeness of His death, certainly we shall be also in the likeness of His resurrection, knowing this, that our old self was crucified with Him, that our body of sin might be done away with, that we should no longer be slaves to sin; for he who has died is freed from sin. Now if we have died with Christ, we believe that we shall also live with Him, knowing that Christ, having been raised from the dead, is never to die again; death no longer is master over Him. For the death that He died, He died to sin, once for all; but the life that He lives, He lives to God. Even so consider yourselves to be dead to sin, but alive to God in Christ Jesus (Rom. 6:1-11).

Can we grasp the great impact of Paul's words? He begins by stating that if one is dead, sin's power and dominion no longer hold sway. Quite reasonable! When we die, we will have no problem with sin. Yet, if we are dead, we will be of no value to Christ's service on earth. If we could only be dead and alive at the same time, that would solve our dilemma. Unthinkable, we say—at least so it seems from our human perspective. Has anyone ever seen any living dead people? Right here, however, Paul startles us with a significant statement. He projects the principle that because of our identification with Jesus Christ, whereby believers have been made one with Him, Christians have shared in the Lord's death and resurrection.

Dead to Sin

Our union with Christ initiated at salvation not only provides forgiveness of sins, it also means we have died with Christ to sin through our faith union with the crucified Lord. In the spiritual sense—yet in a very real way—when Christ died on the cross, we died with Him. When He gained the victory over sin by His blood, we shared in that victory by death. Therefore, our old nature must be seen by faith as dead, truly dead, crucified with Christ. We have become new people. That is exactly what Paul said. As "unreasonable" as it may appear, we must recognize that our "old self" has actually been crucified with Christ. This fact seems most difficult to grasp yet the Bible clearly teaches it. And we must take God at His word; no option remains on that point. Simply because our limited rationalism struggles with the concept, that does not eradicate what the Bible says. The "old self" truly shared in Jesus' crucifixion and thus must be seen as dead and buried with Christ. How can that possibly be? we ask. Jesus died centuries ago and I am alive today. But remember, God transcends time. For God, everything in the entire course of history is "now." So we simply believe God and accept His Word—it is more sure than our finite rationalization.

All this means that we must not slip into the rut of thinking that as Christians we have two equally powerful natures, one good and one bad. *No, the old self has been crucified with Christ.* Our new nature, our regenerated self, now can reign supreme. Eros, as it were, is dethroned. That gets to the heart of what Paul meant when he said, "I have been crucified with Christ; and it is no longer I who live, but Christ lives in me; and the life which I now live in the flesh I live by faith in the Son of God, who loved me, and delivered Himself up for me" (Gal. 2:20).

We Are Alive to God

Not only have we died with Christ and shared in His experience of death, we have also been spiritually resurrected with Him. Do not forget, God is above our time limits. It could well happen by His miraculous power, and it did. Being "in Christ" when He arose, we, too, broke the bondage of death and came forth from the tomb. We now live because Jesus Christ lives. We are now animated by the resurrected life of our Lord in the person of the Holy Spirit. The gift of a whole new nature in Christ has become ours; we have become a resurrected people, born again, dead to sin and alive to God. As Paul wrote, "Therefore if any man is in Christ, he is a new creature; the old things passed away; behold, new things have come" (2 Cor. 5:17). Can sin thus lord it over us? It absolutely cannot. We are dead to the "old" and living the "new" resurrected life of Christ. Our birthright in Jesus Christ guarantees that. As one writer expressed it, we must see ourselves "born crucified." We really have become a "new creation."

The reasoning behind these realities rests in the fact that God visualizes His children as *in Christ* already, seated in heavenly places (Eph. 1:3). Because of our union with Christ we have been elevated to the very heavenlies. The biblical expression "in Christ," or its equivalent, is used over 160 times in the New Testament in Paul's writings alone. Believers literally live *in*

Christ, in true spiritual union with Him, identified with and in Him. Christians are "fused" into Christ as it were. In a spiritual sense, when Christ ascended and took His rightful place on the heavenly throne, so did we "in Him" (Eph. 1:20). As someone has succinctly expressed it, "One of the biggest surprises we are going to experience when we get to heaven is to discover we are already there." And remember, the spiritual is more *real* than the material (2 Cor. 4:18). He resides in us, and we *in Him*—that is our eternal reality, not a mere passing temporal one. And, we have it *now.* This glorious eternal life we already possess. This means that what Christ has experienced, Christians have also experienced in Him. Therefore, when Jesus died, if we are true believers, we were crucified with Him, thus dead to sin. When Jesus broke the bonds of death at His resurrection, we too arose in Him (Eph. 2:6). Paul made this very clear throughout his epistles—we are to believe it. Thus we see ourselves freed from sin's power in Christ. Sin no longer reigns as master; we have been crucified with Christ (Gal. 2:20). We walk in "newness of life." The concept of "in Christ" thus becomes the key that unlocks the treasure-house of the apostle's understanding of the entire Christian experience. Because we are in Christ we are in love. As Drummond so aptly stated, "'Love never faileth.' Love is success, love is happiness, love is life. 'Love,' I say with Browning, 'is energy of life'" (p. 35).

These facts obviously do not appeal to human logic. To realize these truths as we objectively look at our real selves demands dynamic faith. The problem is we still have our old nature to contend with, even though it has been dethroned in Christ. It is there to be sure, but it no longer need reign supreme. Before our conversion, our minds became completely accustomed to moving in accord with the "carnal self." But now they can be constantly renewed by realizing that we have a new nature, a new "mind." We all thought and acted as people of the flesh before being saved, because we were. But now in Christ we can think and act as new people, because we are. Of course, it takes the grace of God to change our old carnal way of thinking, feeling, willing, being—which makes up the essential function of the "mind" as the Bible uses that term. Thus Paul emphasized continually: "Do not be conformed to this world, but be transformed by the *renewing of your mind*" (Rom. 12:2, emphasis added); and to be "renewed in the spirit of your *mind*, and put on the new self, which in the likeness of God has been created in righteousness and holiness of the truth" (Eph. 4:23-24, emphasis added). He stressed, "Have this *mind* among yourselves, which is yours in Christ Jesus" (Phil. 2:5 RSV, emphasis added). Finally, the apostle urges the Philippian believers, "Whatever is true, . . . pure, . . . lovely, . . . let your *mind* dwell on these things" (Phil. 4:8, emphasis added). As the Old Testament writer put it: "For as he *thinks* within himself, so he is" (Prov. 23:7, emphasis added). The mind, the core of conscious acting, plays a central role in our entire being and is to be dealt with by the renewing power of the Holy Spirit. This mind-renewing, faith-transforming, life-changing process the Bible calls *sanctification*. It launches us on a lifelong journey.

Now only faith can grasp all these tremendous truths of what it means to be in Christ. That's why the Christian treads the "path of trust." But *therein lies the victory*. As one author has pointedly expressed it:

> When Christ died on the cross to sin, we were identified with Him in that death to sin. That is, we died with Him. By our union with Him in His death, we were freed from sin and the penalty of sin and emancipated from the power of sin. All our sanctification, therefore, must be traced to, and rest upon, the atoning sacrifice of our Lord Jesus Christ. The cross of Christ is the efficient cause of deliverance from the power of sin. Freedom from the dominion of sin is a blessing we may claim by faith, just as we accept pardon.[2]

The concept can be further illustrated in this way: There are two laws that clamor for ascendancy in the Christian's life. The Bible calls one the "law of sin and of death" (Rom. 8:2). That law operates through the unrenewed mind, the eros-seeking remnant of the "old self." This law of sin dominates if we give it ascendancy through lack of surrender to and faith in Jesus Christ and His Word, thus failing to recognize and claim by faith that our "old self" is dead in Christ. The other law Paul terms the "law of the Spirit of life in Christ Jesus" (Rom. 8:2). This law works through our new, redeemed, resurrected nature as the Holy Spirit constantly renews and enlarges our minds to claim all that God says concerning our total being. In this latter law lies the victory.

We can liken the interaction of these two principles to ascending into the skies in a balloon. The law of sin functions like the law of gravity. Its pull cannot be escaped. Still, the balloon ascends. How? Because of a higher law counteracting the law of gravity. The gas in the balloon has more power than the downward pull of gravity. In like fashion, the "law of the Spirit of life in Christ Jesus" takes its place in our lives by faith as the higher law and consequently overcomes the downward tendency of the unrenewed mind. As we *trust* the Holy Spirit to implement the higher law in our lives, we can ascend to spiritual heights. As the new nature ascends, our minds are constantly renewed into Christlikeness and love. Paul put it very succinctly when he said, "There is therefore now no condemnation for those who are in Christ Jesus. For the law of the Spirit of life in Christ Jesus has set you free from the law of sin and of death" (Rom. 8:1-2). Moreover, the wind of the Spirit carries us along over obstacles in the way God would have us to travel. It can all be summed up in what has been called the exchanged life.

The Exchanged Life

In the entire Christian walk, achieving victory over temptations, fruit-bearing, loving, ministering, and so forth, we must realize that Christ *Himself* becomes formed in the believer by the power of the Holy Spirit (Gal. 4:19). This wonderful truth has already been set forth. It simply means that Christian consecration should never be seen as merely mimicking Jesus. The Holy Spirit actually forms Christ's own life within as He gains expression through the surrendered, victorious life of faith. Strictly speaking, believers must never strive humanistically to be an *imitation* of Christ. Attempting to imitate Jesus in one's own strength can soon degenerate into legalism if not outright humanism. Rather, we must recognize ourselves as an *embodiment* of our lovely Lord. Let it again be said, we rest in union—oneness—with Him. For that reason God can glorify Himself, because only in living out that blessed reality by faith does the Christian reflect His Son and hence bear His fruit. In a word, we live the exchanged life, the new Christ-life for the old self-life; crucified and resurrected with Jesus.

The principle of the exchanged life can be described as an exchange of the eros life for the agape life. Oswald Chambers expressed it this way: "All that Christ wrought for me on the Cross is wrought in me. The free committal of myself to God gives the Holy Spirit the chance to impart to me the holiness of Jesus Christ." Thus Paul admonished the Ephesian believers, "Lay aside the old self . . . and put on the new self" (Eph. 4:22-24).

In that way, and in that way alone, do we become truly Christlike, because Jesus lives His own life through us and hence bears His fruit of love. As one author worded it, Christian living is not our living with Christ's help, it is Christ living His life in us. Willpower does not change men . . . Christ does. Paul expressed it this way: "not I, but Christ" (Gal. 2:20 KJV). Therefore, that portion of our lives that does not reflect His living is not Christian living in the biblical sense, and that portion of our service that is not His doing is not true Christian service. The genuine Christian life and service possess a supernatural and spiritual source. This is the exchanged life. The apostle Paul put it so powerfully when he said, Christ is "our life" (Col. 3:4). Therefore, "For to me, to live is Christ" (Phil. 1:21). Consequently, the love of Christ that abides in us in His own Person becomes the fulfilling of the Law, the primary principle being the exchanged life that centers in "rest," a rest of faith. Martin Luther said, "Therefore, we must nestle under the wings of this mother hen, and not rashly fly away trusting in the powers of our own faith, lest the hawk speedily tear us in pieces and devour us."

Therein resides the clue to victory and the obedience that follows. We stay on the ground of a surrendered faith because of our oneness in and with Christ, continually walking with and abiding in Christ, and letting His life of beauty and love be lived through us as we exchange by faith His life for our old self. Then the marvelous fruit of love flourishes. As one commentator well said:

> Wherever fruit is borne, which pleases the vinedresser and is sweet to his taste, this hangs upon the branches, but it is the vine which bears both the branches and the fruit, and penetrates them with its sap. All the holy thoughts, words, and works of the Christian, which, made sweet by the taste of love, delight God, are altogether fruit of the branches which remain in the vine, with the vine's living sap in them, are altogether gifts received from the abundance of Christ, who is the heart's treasure of love, the mouth's spice of love, the hand's power of love.[3]

Thus, we grow into a manifestation of Christ and His love that brings honor and glory to God who redeemed us.

What About Our Will?

Does this resting in faith in our position in Christ mean we do not exercise our will and determine to serve God with zeal? Emphatically not! Paul climaxed his outline of the in-Christ motif of Romans 6:1-11 by saying in verses 11-12: "Even so consider yourselves to be dead to sin, but alive to God in Christ Jesus. Therefore do not let sin reign in your mortal body that you should obey its lusts." This means that we strongly exercise our will, but it is an exercise of faith in our position in Christ, not a mere human effort to do better. Consequently, we will strive to obey our Lord Jesus Christ as never before. But the quality will be different, it will be a struggle of faith, not of the flesh. The battle now centers on our claiming our position in Christ, not attempting to fight sin in our own strength. And that makes all the difference. It is a totally different brand of warfare, and it yields totally different results. It gives victory.

Furthermore, may it be emphasized one more time, these principles do *not* imply perfectionism. We will always have our sinful nature to contend with until we get to heaven. We find ourselves in an already-and-not-yet spiritual state. That is, God already sees us as complete in Christ, but we will not experience absolute completion until we stand before our Lord at the resurrection (Eph. 4:13). Moreover, living the Spirit-filled, fruit-bearing, exchanged life certainly does not mean that one turns in on oneself and concentrates on how to be blessed personally. Never! That pitfall should be avoided *at all costs*. It is about bearing the fruit of obedience and love for God's glory alone.

The Practicalities

The in-Christ, exchanged-life principle works beautifully in our everyday obedient life as the Holy Spirit actualizes it in practical experience. For example, let us say that we are confronted by one of our old besetting weaknesses. The unrenewed mind, accustomed to foster the things of the flesh, exerts itself. "Here we go again," we say. The battle to overcome the temptation has been fought and lost so often. But now we recognize that the temptation has its appeal because of the old, yet unrenewed part of our lives. That old self still tempts us to think, feel, and decide contrary to God's purpose. But then the truth of the Bible, our identification with Christ, gets pressed home to our consciousness by the Holy Spirit. Realizing our union with Christ in His death and resurrection, and by faith in that biblical reality, we confront the temptation and in essence retort: *This sin no longer has compelling power over me. I am dead to it. I am a new person. The old nature has been crucified with Christ. I am alive to God, and the resurrected life of Jesus Christ has become my new nature.* Thus, we exercise our will and take the ground of faith and stand against the temptation on the basis of those realities. Believing Christ's promise, by faith we then look to our living God and His power for the victory. Faith in the fact of one's death to sin, and a vital look in faith to God, constitutes the answer. That act of faith involves the twin aspects of the grounds for belief—the written Word of God and our powerful Lord, the Living Word of God.

A battle rages, of course. But again let it be stressed, the battle does not involve fighting sin directly. That will spell certain defeat. Sin always exerts itself stronger than we in our human ability are able to cope. We dare not fight Satan on his own ground. His power can invariably send us on retreat and defeat. The war to be fought and the consequential exercise of our wills centers in striving to stay on *the field of faith.* The battle is the Lord's (2 Chron. 20:15). There, with faith in God's promise and power, we stand. How Satan and sin love to deceive us here! The flesh will also hoodwink us. The world, the devil, and the flesh will do anything and everything to get us to surrender our faith regarding our position in Christ. As one author has put it: "His aim is to get the believer to forsake faith's position . . . for the moment the believer quits faith's position, he falls under Satan's power. Hence the fight is not merely 'the good fight' . . . but the good fight *of faith*" (1 Tim. 6:12, emphasis added).[4]

So we take our stand on faith—faith in the fact that we are dead to sin and alive to God in Christ. We have an exchanged life. We look to God for His power to overcome. In faith's way we defeat "the wiles of the devil" (Eph. 6:11 kjv) and become victorious. Satan was defeated at the Cross. He is a defeated foe. We do not work *toward* victory; by faith we work *from* it as already ours in Christ. Not only in eternity will we be delivered from the penalty and presence of sin, now by faith we are saved from its devastating power. This quality of living should not to be thought of as unusual for the Christian. It is the normal Christian life, normal according to New Testament principles. Being crucified with Christ and raised to walk in newness of life must never be seen as a position one attains by ardent spiritual striving, that is, the end result of much maturing and gigantic growing in Christ. All believers hold this marvelous position by virtue of the fact of being born again by the grace of God and possessed by the Holy Spirit. We need to know that we are accepted by God in Christ and a whole new nature has been given us. Therefore, we permit the Holy Spirit to renew our minds constantly, and sanctification follows. Redemption rests as much in the present tense as in the past or the future. All of this assures obedience. That is why the hymn writer said:

> When we walk with the Lord
> In the light of *His Word*
> What a glory He sheds on our way! . . .
> *Trust and obey,* for there's no other way
> To be happy in Jesus, but to *trust and obey.*
>   (emphasis added)

John was right: "This is the victory that has overcome the world—our faith" (1 John 5:4).

What a wonderful reality! We ought never to permit ourselves to be maneuvered off the ground of faith and again start striving in the flesh. But make no mistake about it, to remain on faith's ground demands discipline. This follows because the secret of standing on the ground of faith revolves around learning to abide in Christ. Therefore, as Griffith Thomas expressed it, "Let all your enthusiasm be put into abiding." That spells victory, and victory spells obedience, and that results in love.

Furthermore, our gracious God has given us another source of strength for obedience that leads to love. Paul calls it the "whole armor of God" (Eph. 6:11 KJV). Every soldier needs equipment to fight successfully. In achieving victory in Christ, the same reality holds.

The Resources of the Christian Armor

Paul shares what the whole armor of God consists of:

> Finally, be strong in the Lord, and in the strength of His might. Put on the full armor of God, that you may be able to stand firm against the schemes of the devil. For our struggle is not against flesh and blood, but against the rulers, against the powers, against the world forces of this darkness, against the spiritual forces of wickedness in the heavenly places. Therefore, take up the full armor of God, that you may be able to resist in the evil day, and having done everything, to stand firm. Stand firm therefore, having girded your loins with truth, and having put on the breastplate of righteousness, and having shod your feet with the preparation of the gospel of peace; in addition to all, taking up the shield of faith with which you will be able to extinguish all the flaming missiles of the evil one. And take the helmet of salvation, and the sword of the Spirit, which is the word of God (Eph. 6:10-17).

Each piece of the Christian's protective armor assumes an essential role for victory in the life of obedient love. First, believers must be girded about "with truth." This means living lives of genuine honesty. Whenever any Christians get "unreal" about themselves or about their situation, they open themselves to the devil's attack. Girding centers in integrity in all situations, telling the truth. We have seen that this makes up one aspect of the fruit of love (Gal. 5:22-23).

Then, Christian believers should strap on the "breastplate of righteousness." The Scriptures present righteousness in a twofold sense. Believers are *declared* righteous in God's sight because of their faith in Jesus Christ (Rom. 4:3, 9). Theologians call that gracious gift "forensic justification." That is to say, God imputes—or puts to one's account—the righteousness of Christ (Rom. 4:6). But one also *becomes* righteous in Christian living by the power and work of the indwelling of the Holy Spirit. The Spirit continually works, making believers more ethically and morally righteous through His mighty power. We are never saved by our works (Eph. 2:8-9), but our works reflect our salvation (Eph. 2:10).

Look at the Christian's "new shoes." Paul says one should be shod with the "preparation of the gospel of peace." The word *preparation* literally means "making one fully ready to plunge into the fight." The paradox in Paul's statement is quite fascinating; the preparation implies a *battle,* but the weapon is the "gospel of *peace*." Christians wage a war with the weapons of peace, the marvelous *peace of God* contained in God's Good News. Jesus said, "Blessed are the peacemakers, for they shall be called sons of God" (Matt. 5:9). Believers battle, but they battle with the invincible weapon of God's peace. In the final analysis, this is the only way to wage war if one wishes to win it for the Savior.

Paul further urges believers to put on the "helmet of salvation." For a soldier, lugging that heavy steel helmet around all day may seem a chore during the dreary, strenuous hours of basic training. But when the bullets start flying, that helmet becomes a soldier's best friend. When one leaps out of the trenches and onto the spiritual battlefield, one had best be sure that the head, the most vital part of the body, is safely covered in the salvation that God alone can give. Simply put, if one feels uncertain about his or her salvation, tremendous vulnerability to Satan's arrows becomes a certainty. Furthermore, Satan knows exactly where to aim his fiery darts. But God has a piece of equipment to handle those darts.

Paul tells us that we should also take up the "sword of the Spirit," the Word of God. The Scriptures become the believer's powerful offensive weapon. This is akin to the gospel of peace. To repeat an old cliche: The best defense is a good offense. The Bible never pictures the believers as standing with their backs to the wall, frantically defending the fort. Jesus said, "I will build My church; and the gates of Hades shall not overpower it" (Matt. 16:18). The picture painted is not that of the Christian holed up in some citadel hanging on until Jesus comes. The church takes the offensive and storms the stronghold of sin, Satan, and evil. The people of God have enlisted in an offensive victorious army, and their primary weapon is the Word of God.

Finally, and of most importance, God has given us the ever available "shield of faith." Christians can never be secure without that defensive—and offensive—weapon. So, we find ourselves back on the ground of *faith* once again if we expect to enjoy victory in spiritual battles. As we exercise faith in our identification with Christ in our death and resurrection in Him, victory over Satan's fiery arrows is assured. But all this has surely become amply evident by now. Moreover, it all implies that the obedient life is well worth living.

The Blessings of Obedience

Obedience reaps rewards, and the blessings are remarkably like love. To begin with, obeying God brings deep, inner satisfaction. To put Christ first in one's decision making proves a true delight. Peace and joy—products of agape love—pervade the obedient heart.

Further, to be found in God's will guarantees finding purpose in life. Deep in the human psyche rests the desire for goals, purpose, meaning, and reality. These sterling qualities can only be discovered by being found in the center of our Lord's will. Obedience and God's rich blessings go hand in glove.

Our creator God knows what is best for us. To obey Him in all things will assure us of the best in life and our being amply cared for. Paul wrote, "And my God shall supply all your needs according to His riches in glory in Christ Jesus" (Phil. 4:19). This does not necessarily mean "health and wealth," but it does mean contentment. Obedience teaches us "to be content in whatever circumstances . . . to get along with humble means, and . . . how to live in prosperity; in any and every circumstance . . . being filled and going hungry, both of having abundance and suffering need" (Phil. 4:11-12). Love is longsuffering and patient because it is obedient.

Relationships with people actually depend on the depth of our obedience to Christ. We cannot be contentious, easily provoked, demanding, and selfish and say at the same time that we are obedient to our Lord. Obeying God means relating in love to our fellows. Positive, productive fellowship grows out of agape. John said, "What we have seen and heard we proclaim to you also, that you also may have fellowship with us; and indeed our fellowship is with the Father, and with His Son Jesus Christ. And these things we write, so that our joy may be made complete" (1 John 1:3-4). Such a fellowship of obedience is complete joy—a fruit of love.

Additionally, following God with the whole heart divorces us from love of the world. We are not to "love the world" (1 John 2:15). John goes so far as to say, "If anyone loves the world, the love of the Father is not in him" (1 John 2:15). This orientation saves us from the world that "is passing away;" only the obedient, "the one who does the will of God abides forever" (1 John 2:17). What a great grasp of life!

Then, the obedient believer lives a life that contributes. What is life worth if we do not make a positive contribution during our days? Just to live is meaningless and empty. To live a contributing life makes it all worthwhile. Eros fails; agape wins.

Finally, obedience brings glory to God. Our first parents, Adam and Eve, failed in the Garden of Eden. They disobeyed the Lord. Not only did they personally suffer (and we as well because of our solidarity with them), but God's plan for creation was thwarted. Thanks be to the gracious God who has redeemed us and given us a new opportunity to obey Him. And obeying will bring glory to God and His redeeming grace.

Obedient love does have great rewards. And though we fail at times, there is *in Christ* a life of victory to be experienced. How marvelous is God's love to us that has moved us into a life of obedience and equipped and enabled us to experience it. That really strikes at what life is all about.

So, clothed with the full armor of God, brandishing the sword of the Spirit, and resting in faith in Christ, believers invade enemy territory and go forth from victory to victory in the name of Jesus Christ. Into this glorious and triumphant battle we are all called. The promise of being a conqueror in Christ makes obedience a glowing reality. And obeying God reflects our deep love for Him. "Therefore, my beloved brethren, be steadfast, immovable, always abounding in the work of the Lord, knowing that your toil is not in vain in the Lord" (1 Cor. 15:58). That is obedience; and obedience is love.

Endnotes

1. C. S. Lewis, *Mere Christianity* (New York: Touchstar Books, 1996), 115.
2. Steven Barabas, *So Great Salvation* (New York: Revell), 88-89.
3. R. C. H. Lenski, *The Interpretation of St. John's Gospel* (Minneapolis: Augsburg, 1963), 103.
4. Evan Hopkins, *The Law of Liberty in the Spiritual Life* (Philadelphia: Sunday School Times, 1995), 108.

6

Love Serves

Through love serve one another.

Galatians 5:13

D oes love mean service, even sacrificed service? Unquestionably! Picking up on Paul's thread of thought shared in the previous chapter, he tells us: "The love of Christ controls us" (2 Cor. 5:14). The conclusion cannot be avoided that loving Christ controls us and thus makes us contributing Christians. Agape love requires that we engage in the service of our Lord. Many passages of Scripture parallel Paul's word, making this principle paramount. Our Lord Himself set the classic example. The Bible says, "Christ also loved the church and gave Himself up for her" (Eph. 5:25). Jesus' love moved Him to serve the church even unto death. John goes on to admonish believers, "But whoever has the world's goods, and beholds his brother in need and closes his heart against him, how does the love of God abide in him? Little children, let us not love with word or with tongue, but in deed and in truth" (1 John 3:17-18).

In other words, if we love God with all of our heart and thus move into a life of experiencing the greatest thing in the world, we must lovingly engage in the service and ministry of Jesus Christ. *Loving* God and our fellows means lovingly *serving* God and our fellows. What a privilege that is. As Drummond put it, "Take into your new sphere of labor, where you also mean to lay down your life, that simple charm (of love), and your life work must succeed. You can take nothing greater, you need take nothing less" (p. 33).

Serving God invariably involves much of what has already

been suggested in the previous chapters. Ministry revolves around the faith-love motif of the Christian experience. That is to say, we serve because of our love and devotion to Jesus Christ. All effective and useful Christian service becomes a venture of faith. We have learned that faith fosters the victory that overcomes the world in our personal struggles; faith also brings the victory that overcomes the world as we invade that world with the gospel of Jesus Christ. This has always been true, it always shall be true, and the unfolding history of the Church demonstrates this fact time and again.

A Classic Example of Serving in Faith and Love

One of the most magnificent works of faith and love in Henry Drummond's day was epitomized in the ministry of George Müller of Bristol, England. Müller tirelessly served Christ, caring for thousands of orphans in needy Britain in the 1800s. The Müller saga stands as one of the most beautiful stories of loving service that one can read.

The inspiration for Müller's work came when he saw an orphanage work at the city of Halle, in old Prussia. In Bristol, Müller felt the Lord leading him to begin a similar work. He wanted to give a testimony to the world that the Lord still hears and answers prayer in response to loving service and faith. God always meets that commitment.

Müller began his labors in Bristol in 1832. At that time, he served as co-pastor with a fellow minister, Mr. Craik, at Gideon and Bethesda Chapels. The membership of the churches quadrupled in a very short time and pictured a ministry of sacrificial love; neither man received a salary. Müller continued to preach in Bristol even after he began his orphanage work. At the time of his death, he had a congregation of two thousand worshipers at Bethesda Chapel.

In 1834, Mr. Müller founded the Scripture Knowledge Institution for Home and Abroad. This work went on through

Müller's life. During his lifetime, 122,000 persons had been taught in schools supported by his efforts, along with 282,000 Bibles and 1,500,000 Testaments distributed. Also, 112,000,000 religious books, pamphlets, and tracts had been circulated, and missionaries ministered all over the globe.

When Müller became seventy years old, he began to make evangelistic tours. During this time he traveled 200,000 miles, going around the world. He preached in many countries and in several different languages. Three times he traveled and preached throughout the United States. He continued his evangelistic ministry to the age of ninety. During those years of evangelistic work he spoke to three million people. All his expenses were met in answer to the prayer of faith.

Yet all agree that of Müller's undertakings, the orphanages of Bristol became his greatest labor of love and faith. He began that work with only two shillings, but being a man of deep commitment and prayer, he received the funds necessary to build buildings, feed and clothe orphans, and meet the needs of thousands for some sixty years. Müller never asked for one penny. Yet, in all that time the children never missed a meal. Müller said that if they ever had to go without a meal, he would take it as evidence that the Lord did not want the work to continue. He did not mean to tempt God, he simply had that sort of faith. For example, on one occasion the "cupboard was bare," not a scrap of food could be found for breakfast for the hundreds of hungry orphans. A fellow worker came to Müller's room that early morning to tell him the children should be kept in bed as there was no food. "Get them up and to the dining hall," Müller retorted. "But we have no food," replied the worker. "Get them up and assembled," Müller insisted. The worker acquiesced. All the children rose, dressed, and went to their tables in the dining hall. George Müller stood up and in prayer asked God's blessings on their meal—but they had no meal. As the great man of faith finished his prayer with a hearty

"Amen," the doors of the dining hall suddenly burst open and a cadre of people rushed in, their arms loaded with groceries. *God honors faith*.

Müller learned early that to trust the Lord for a shilling proved as difficult as to trust Him for a thousand pounds. But trust he did. Funds for one project after another came in as answers to prayer. Six hundred pounds a week were required for the support of the orphans at the time of Müller's death. And the Lord provided day by day.

The George Müller story reveals some vital realities about the agape life. Two characteristics, as Müller demonstrated, inevitably lead to the summit of effective service: (1) God's people are to serve Him with love and zest and effectiveness; and (2) they must develop a fervent prayer life. In short, God uses people of agape love and faith and makes them contributing Christians. Several reasons can be found to demonstrate these realities.

Serving the World's Needs

In the first place, the Christian service of love becomes the only hope for our desperate world. Our Lord said that Christians are "the salt of the earth" (Matt. 5:13). As salt flavors, purifies, and preserves, the believer exemplifies similar spiritual qualities. Christ expects His people to permeate society with a flavoring, purifying, preserving influence.

Something of a *flavoring quality* should constantly radiate from the child of God. D. L. Moody was preaching to a great congregation in a large hall. On the wall hung a huge billboard with the text: "God is love" (1 John 4:8). Moody pointed to the sign and said, "God is love! I believe that in any great city, thousands would be converted if they only believed the truth that 'God is love.'"

Moody struck the right note. If people could only grasp how Christ loves them, many would surely be moved to the Lord. But how will they believe? What will bring them to this knowledge?

Perhaps a few will be reached by reading posters and roadside signs to that effect. But not too many will believe by merely reading. What about preaching? Will this convert the entire world? True, many, who hear the preaching of God's love, believe. But millions more never come near a church or turn on a religious program where the love of God is forthrightly proclaimed through the media. What about them?

Only one way surfaces by which the mass of humanity will come to know and understand that God is love and hence be drawn to our loving Lord. It will happen when God's own people become filled to overflowing with the love of Christ and engage in sacrificial service to them. Then, and then alone, will the whole world understand the glorious truth of God's compassion. The world needs to see a *living demonstration* that God is love. Being the salt of the earth demands such. When God's people become filled with the Holy Spirit and transformed into people of loving ministry, they *flavor* their entire sphere of influence with the love of Christ. The impact that the first century church made on the watching world can be summed up in Luke's words in Acts 2:47 when he tells us that the believers were "having favor with all the people. And the Lord was adding to their number day by day those who were being saved." That makes up a central part of being the salt of the earth. But do not forget Jesus' warning, "If the salt has become tasteless, . . . It is good for nothing anymore, except to be thrown out and trampled under foot by men" (Matt. 5:13).

Salt also has a *purifying quality.* That characteristic should mark the loving Christian life. Previously we mentioned Bertha Smith, missionary to China. She exemplified the purifying quality of salt. Few could ever be the same after having been in fellowship with Bertha. Her life so touched others that they lived more pure lives. God wants all His people to purify others by their own purity, beauty, and love. That too becomes a vital part of being the salt of the earth.

Finally, *salt preserves.* How different communities become because of the influence of the loving church! Schools, hospitals, children's homes, and a multitude of other great benevolent services found their inceptions in Spirit-filled churches. For example, during the great prayer awakening in the middle of the nineteenth century, hundreds of American Christian colleges were instituted by awakened evangelicals. Nothing preserves society like the loving church.

The principle of preservation can be seen on an individual basis also. The vital ministry of personal witnessing for Christ, for instance, enables a Christian to become the "salt of the earth." In sharing the Good News of the Lord Jesus with others, and leading them to personal faith and commitment to Christ, people are preserved to eternal life. We shall see this principle in greater depth later in this chapter.

Thus, all who believe and love become the salt of the earth. But, remember, if salt loses its taste, it is good for nothing. This reeling world desperately needs the ministry of Christians. It will never be flavored, purified, or preserved unless believers permit the love of Christ to move them into their rightful stance in service and salt it.

Serving to Glorify God

Moreover, sincere service personifies and demonstrates God's love; thus bringing honor to our Lord. Seeking God's glory and honor always sets the foundation of the Christian's motive. When Paul entered Athens and saw their idolatry, their ignorance, and their disregard for the knowledge of the true God, "his spirit was being provoked within him as he was beholding the city full of idols" (Acts 17:16). Divine jealousy stirred the apostle. He was deeply moved with emotion that the name of Jesus should be honored. As one stated, "He burned with longing that the Athenians should know and honor the God they either ignorantly worshiped or actually by their idolatry denied."[1] So Paul courageously declared Christ in the marketplace or wherever anyone would listen. God's honor stood at stake. The Shorter Catechism expresses it: "Man's chief end is to glorify God, and to enjoy Him for ever." The whole purpose for living centers in magnifying the name of Jesus Christ. That is why we love. That is why we serve.

Serving to Further the Kingdom

Jesus taught us to pray:

> Our Father who art in heaven,
> Hallowed be Thy name.
> Thy kingdom come,
> Thy will be done,
> On earth as it is in heaven (Matt. 6:9-10).

Through love—manifesting itself in properly motivated ministry—we actually further God's kingdom. In a very real sense, we can be a partial answer to our own prayers. That generates life at its best. Loving service brings purpose and meaning into each day. Love makes spiritual, psychological, practical sense.

Of course all true believers attempt to serve Christ, at least in some way. At the same time, however, most have had some frustrating experiences in Christian service. Why do our feverish efforts so often seem to accomplish little? Perhaps the reason for the seeming failure in much Christian service arises because of the attempt to serve God and extend His kingdom in a way that the Holy Spirit does not direct. If such be the case, one can hardly expect God's blessings or the Spirit's power. God's work must be done in God's way. Mere activity alone will never suffice. How then can one be assured of serving Christ according to God's plan?

Serving God His Way

Many figures of speech in the New Testament describe the people of God. The Scriptures picture the church as the bride of Christ, God's vineyard, God's flock, God's building, a holy priesthood, the new Israel, and a holy nation. Perhaps the most graphic analogy, however, presents the church as a *body*. It surely seems to be the favorite of Paul when he presents God's people as servants. It makes sense: What does a body do? It moves, functions, and acts—it works. Simply expressed, the serving local church ministers as a functioning *body* of Christ. This approach to the service of a church has important implications.

Some Important Implications

First, as a body has different parts with different functions, so does a local church in its ministry. To say that all members of a congregation are the same and therefore do the same thing in service misses the point. Abilities, gifts, talents, and ministries vary with each member. The Holy Spirit does not create cookie-cutter Christians. Paul asked rhetorically, "All are not apostles, are they? All are not prophets, are they? All are not teachers, are they? All are not workers of miracles, are they? All do not have gifts of healings, do they? All do not speak with tongues, do they? All do not interpret, do they?" (1 Cor. 12:29-30). He explained, "For even as the body is one and yet has many members, and all the members of the body, though they are many, are one body, so also is Christ. For by one Spirit we were all baptized into one body" (1 Cor. 12:12-13). A diversity of members and corresponding functions make up a healthy, serving church body. After all, a church faces a diversity of needs; therefore, a diversity of ministries is called for. This necessitates diversity among the serving members of the body.

Second, the metaphor of the body further suggests that in the church's diversity there remains a central, inescapable spiritual unity. A true body of Christ always manifests itself as a single unit. This means that all the members stand equal and one before God. All are engaged in the one overall task of kingdom progress. The responsibility in Christian ministry becomes incumbent upon every member of the church body. The commission to serve God has been given to the entire body. Stott again reminds us, "The essential unity of the Church, originating in the call of God and illustrated in the metaphors of the Scripture, lead us to this conclusion: the responsibilities which God has entrusted to His Church He has entrusted to His *Whole Church.*"[2] In other words, God sees every Christian serving as a member of the unified, diversified body of Christ. God allows no exemptions. No "lame legs" or "withered arms" have a place in Christ's serving body. The church fulfills its purpose only when every member gives of themselves in love to worship and the service of Christ; the so-called clergy and laity alike.

A hard line between the clergy and lay members of the church cannot be found in the Bible. Such a line distorts the New Testament picture. In the Scriptures, the laity are the whole people of God, and the clergy have the privilege of oversight, shepherding and equipping them for service. Paul brings this out very clearly in Ephesians 4:11-12: "And He gave some as apostles, and some as prophets, and some as evangelists, and some as pastors and teachers, for the equipping of the saints for the work of service, to the building up of the body of Christ." But in unity of spirit all serve, leaders and laity alike, because they have all become members of the body. Thus, with the diversified but integrated body, the work of Christ goes forward effectively.

The Key Question

The key question becomes: How can a Christian fit into his or her local church so that the body becomes a healthy, virile, fully functioning body of Christ to serve the world in love? Paul emphatically states that a church becomes a servant church on the basis of the bestowal of spiritual, ministering gifts. That is, God equips all believers for ministry with special service endowments called the gifts of the Spirit (Eph. 4, Rom. 12, 1 Cor. 12). These grace gifts enable a Christian to serve Christ with power and effect. But what are these gifts? Many different—even conflicting—ideas have surfaced concerning the issue.

The gifts of the Spirit must be seen as ministering abilities, bestowed on *every* Christian *for ministry.* They are not given for personal, spiritual indulgence of any kind. The Holy Spirit graciously imparts these gifts so that believers may be effective in their service for the Savior. If this principle is kept constantly in mind, many errors can be sidestepped and emotions defused. God simply gives spiritual gifts so Christians can serve Christ with effect. The gifts contribute to the building up of the body of Christ. That makes up their nature and primary purpose.

What the Bible Says about the Gifts

It is important to distinguish these *gifts* of the Spirit from the *fruit* of the Spirit discussed earlier. The fruit is the manifestation of the Spirit in daily life to develop Christlike love. The gifts are the manifestation of the Holy Spirit through the believer to make loving service effectual. This fact becomes evident in the listing of the gifts of the Spirit enumerated in the Scriptures mentioned above.

First Corinthians 12:8-10 lists the following:
  1. utterance of wisdom
  2. utterance of knowledge
  3. faith
  4. healing
  5. miracles
  6. prophecies

7. discernment of spirits
8. various kinds of tongues
9. interpretation of tongues

In 1 Corinthians 12:28-29, the following are listed:
1. apostles
2. prophets
3. teachers
4. workers of miracles
5. healers
6. helpers
7. administrators
8. speakers in various kinds of tongues

Romans 12:6-8 presents additions to the Corinthian passage:
1. prophecy
2. service
3. teaching
4. exhortation
5. giving
6. aiding
7. mercy

Eliminating the obvious duplications in Paul's passages, nineteen gifts are recorded. From this number, it becomes clear that the entire work of the ministry of Christian service can be fully met in these spiritual gifts.

Clearly, these gifts are important. Paul stressed the significance of the Spirit's ministering gifts, stating: "Now concerning spiritual gifts, brethren, I do not want you to be unaware" (1 Cor. 12:1). Several ideas concerning the gifts need to be explored. First, it becomes obvious that some gifts lay emphasis on Christian personalities who themselves have particular ministries; for example, apostles, prophets, and teachers. In other instances, the emphasis rests upon the function rather than on the gifted individual; for example, faith and varieties of tongues. But this distinction should not be pressed too far, for a gift apart from a believer to exercise the gift becomes meaningless, and a Christian not exercising his or her gift becomes an ineffectual servant of Christ. The gift and the gifted weave the warp and woof of the fabric. We cannot have the one without the other.

Then, the gifts of the Spirit should not be confused with natural talents. Though all people have some natural abilities, abilities that God will surely use in His service, the spiritual gifts are not talents per se. Marcus Dods, the pastor who influenced Henry Drummond so profoundly stated that all believers are endowed "with certain powers which they had not previously possessed and which were due to the influence of the Holy Spirit."[3] Spiritual gifts are *grace bestowals* of the Holy Spirit. Christians do not assume them of their own volition. They are *supernatural* endowments.

Moreover, the gifts should be exercised only under the control of the Holy Spirit. Paul is emphatic about this. They should not be employed simply when and how the believer wishes, let alone selfishly enjoyed. "The operator . . . is always God; every one of the gifts in every person that manifests them . . . is bestowed and set in motion by him."[4]

Finally, realize that all believers have at least one or more spiritual endowments. Paul said, "But to each one of us grace was given according to the measure of Christ's gift" (Eph. 4:7). Make no mistake here, all true Christians are gifted believers. This we have already pointed out. But it should be emphasized because it forms a vital link in service. The practical outcome is: All can serve Jesus Christ in love. The Holy Spirit abides within, not only to lead, direct, empower, and create love, but to enable Christians to serve Jesus Christ faithfully and effectively in and through the life of the church.

Now what actually happens when the gifts are in operation?

The Practical Outworking

The following delineation of the outworking of the spiritual gifts should help us see how these love gifts operate in the total life and ministry of a local church.

✑ for the proclamation of God's self-disclosure: the gift of prophecy or preaching to proclaim God's truth to exhort, comfort, and help people

✑ for teaching the divine revelation: the gift of teaching

✑ for enabling God's blessing to flow into needy lives: the gift of faith that enables believers to rest upon God's promises and trust in the power that is beyond the sphere of human possibilities

✑ for the revelation of God's will and purpose in matters: the gift of wisdom so that God's purpose in His Word may be grasped

✑ for understanding the practical application of eternal principles in daily experience: the utterance of knowledge

✑ for protection against evil: the gift of discernment of spirits

✑ for the practical manifestation of the love of Christ, three gifts: mercy, the Paraclete gift, and giving

✑ for maintaining order in the life and work of the church: the gift of government stresses the importance of church administration

✑ for help in the community: the gift of serviceable ministries or "helps"

✑ as special signs of God's power and presence, four gifts: miracles, healings, tongues, and interpretations of tongues[5]

Some important points come to the fore in this brief outline. First, and obviously, the number of gifts found in the Scriptures is comparatively small—only nineteen or so. This forces one to the conclusion that each gift should be understood as a designation of a *class* of gifts. In each classification there will no doubt be many variations. Circumstances, situations, and needs vary from culture to culture and from generation to generation; hence, the need for variety under differing conditions. And, although the lists in the Bible may seem relatively short, the Spirit still makes full provision for all the needs of a church in its growth, worship, and worldwide ministry. The organization of the local church, its government, its instruction, its equipping, its outreach, and its entire corporate life are fully provided for.

Second, the principle of spiritual gifts makes the local church a true body of Christ. The Holy Spirit bestows the gifts as He wills (1 Cor. 12:11), creating a body that is fully developed and functional. To build any body that is all hands or eyes or feet is a bit ludicrous. The Holy Spirit will always construct a perfectly functioning, well-proportioned, and unified organism. Therefore, all believers will never possess the same gift. It would never be a fully functioning body of Christ if such were the case.

Finally, when gifted church members employ their ministry under the direction of the Holy Spirit, the church grows and the work of the kingdom progresses. As William Barclay states, "The picture we get is the picture of a church vividly alive. Things happened; in fact astonishing things happened. Life was heightened and intensified and sensitised. There was nothing flat and dull and ordinary about the early Church."[6] Furthermore, in the context of ministering one's spiritual gift, the door often opens for an effective witness for Christ to the lost. When we lovingly step into a person's life and meet a genuine need, that person may well listen to the gospel as never before and trust Jesus Christ as Lord and Savior. It must be said, if love is the greatest thing in the world, winning someone to Christ in love is the greatest service in the world. Remember, heaven rejoices over one sinner who repents (Luke 15:7). But how does one discover his or her gift to serve Jesus Christ meaningfully?

How to Discover Your Gift

Guiding principles can be found in the Scriptures and in experience to aid in discovering one's gift. The following ideas constitute a few of the basic spiritual disciplines in uncovering one's Spirit-inspired ministry. They could be called the "Ten Commandments of Discovering Spiritual Gifts."

1. Have confidence that you have one or more. The Bible forthrightly declares that you do.
2. Study the Scriptures: They have the answers to questions on the theme and what God wishes to accomplish in the world through Jesus Christ.
3. Ask: How has God used me in the past, really used me? That may give some clues.
4. Ask: What do spiritual people say? They may provide some answers. Others often understand us better than we do ourselves. Sharing can be most important.
5. Ask: What do I like to do? We like to do what we do well. We should do well in the exercising of our gift.
6. Ask: What needs burden me? God may want you to do that service.
7. Ask: What challenges me; that is, what does the Holy Spirit lay on my heart?
8. Ask: What open doors are before me? What opportunities are present? God may be in it.
9. Rest in Jesus and be open to change.
10. Above all, pray for God's leadership.

Today, desperate needs press in from every side. People everywhere reach out for help, every kind of help. Churches should rise to the challenge. And on the basis of what has been said of a church as a ministering body of Christ, when the principles become implemented in the congregation, it fulfills what Paul meant when he said:

Speaking the truth in love, we are to grow up in all aspects into Him, who is the head, even Christ, from whom the whole body, being fitted and held together by that which every joint supplies, according to the proper working of each individual part, causes the growth of the body for the building up of itself in love (Eph. 4:15-16).

If we are Christians and want to live a life of true love, we have a solemn responsibility before God to step into situations and meet needs. And God has graciously equipped us to do just that. We are all to serve on the basis of our spiritual gift in the body, the church. If agape love means anything, it means getting on with the task of serving our Lord Jesus Christ in and through the gifted church and thereby extending His kingdom on earth. The love life is truly a serving life.

This leads to a most important aspect of ministry that must be emphasized. We have looked at it briefly several times before; now a more extensive look is in order.

A Vital Dimension of Loving Service

In Christ, we have become a gifted people. We have all received a respective, distinct ministry to perform in the body of Christ. But there abides one principle of loving service incumbent on all—no exceptions. The Lord commands it of every believer. Love demands witnessing for Christ. Sharing a word of witness is *not* a gift; it comes to us all as a commandment from our Lord. When Paul said, "The love of Christ controls us" (or as the King James Authorized Version expresses it, "constrains us"), he referred specifically to sharing the gospel to the lost multitudes. If we would reflect the love of God in the most profound sense of ministry and service, it must entail sharing the Good News of the Lord Jesus Christ to those who do not know Him as personal Lord and Savior. Jesus said, "The Son of Man has come to seek and to save that which was lost" (Luke 19:10). Then He added, "As the Father has sent Me, I also send you" (John 20:21). We all know the classic, oft-quoted verse in John's gospel, "For God so loved the world, that He gave His only begotten Son, that whoever believes in Him should not perish, but have eternal life" (3:16). That very fact along with our Lord's commission compels our commitment to evangelize. Loving and sharing Christ by every legitimate means go together. The love of Christ inescapably constrains us to present Christ to a lost and needy world.

This implies a most significant principle. If we would win people to Christ, we must not see them merely as lost souls; they are to be seen in a holistic sense and ministered to in a holistic manner.

Witnessing to the Whole Person

Compartmentalizing life has become a common problem for many of us reared in Western society. Whether we realize it or not, we have been immersed in Greek philosophy due to our cultural and educational background. The Greeks were notorious for cubbyholing the differing aspects of life. We thus seem to chop up our experiences and label them with the implication that one area of life does not really affect the other. But that approach misses the mark—especially the biblical principle of the unified human personality. Labeling one part of human experience "spiritual" and another "mental" and another "secular" and so forth can lead to many errors, not the least being the hindrance it creates in witnessing with relevance and good effect. Make no mistake, salvation invades the person as a whole (Mark 5:24-34). John hinted at this when he wrote, "Little children, let us not love with word or with tongue, but in deed and truth" (1 John 3:18). We serve in deed *and* truth in a holistic manner to the whole person.

Perhaps the most beautiful instance of the principle of ministering to spiritual, physical, social, and psychological needs can be found in Mark's gospel (5:24-34). Mark records how Jesus healed a woman who had been sick for twelve years. The account paints a perfect picture of Christ's complete ministry. Several salient aspects of the encounter emerge, all relevant to effective witnessing.

First, a needy person comes along (v. 25). The woman really suffered with her sickness. She was vividly conscious of that need. We say, why of course she knows it! Yet people are not always aware of their true needs. We must help them see that their deepest need is for Christ. "Sick" persons must become aware of their "illness" and acknowledge it. But we must begin where they are, and minister in any way possible as we touch their entire lives, culminating in pointing them to their most desperate need of Jesus Christ as Lord and Savior.

Second, in the woman's own attempt to deal with her problem, she found herself helpless. She had spent all her resources on physicians and could find healing from none (v. 26). She even grew worse, and was reduced to psychological despair. A feeling of helplessness often serves as a necessary step before one sincerely looks to the Lord as their only hope.

Then, at this point she "heard the reports about Jesus" (v. 27 RSV). Her faith began to take root. Maybe help could be found after all! That seed of faith grew until she finally realized that her problem could be fully met in Jesus Christ. Hearing the reports about Jesus stands as absolutely necessary. "Faith comes from hearing" (Rom. 10:17). We can play a vital role right here.

The woman also recognized that faith must be active; it must reach out (Mark 5:28). "Faith, if it has no works, is dead, being by itself" (James 2:17). So she touched the border of Jesus' garment. She exercised her faith. She did not merely contemplate what Christ could do; she turned in active faith to Him. Vital!

Then the miracle happened. Instantly healing came (Mark 5:29). What a thrill went through her whole personhood. Christ had made her whole. She felt it (v. 29). She knew it.

At that juncture, the Lord asked what seemed to the disciples a ridiculous question: "Who touched my garments?" (v. 30). The disciples responded, "You see the multitude pressing in on You, and You say, 'Who touched Me?'" (v. 31). Yet our Lord knows well when someone touches Him.

The woman realized that she had put herself on the spot. She found herself in a social bind. That she had been healed she doubted not. But now she must confess openly, before others, what Jesus had done for her (v. 32). She trembled. But regardless, she came "fearing and trembling, aware of what had happened to her, . . . and fell down before Him, and told Him the whole truth" (v. 33). Belief and confession are both essential to experience God's full touch (Rom. 10:10).

Finally, our Lord pronounced the great benediction: "Daughter, your faith has made you well; go in peace, and be healed of your affliction" (Mark 5:34). Her faith saved her, but her confession before her peers gave her the Lord's benediction of peace and she experienced the approval of her friends. The whole episode stands as an example that faith saves and that open confession brings the fullness of God's blessings to the total person.

The pattern is now complete. Actually, the entire healing experience beautifully pictures Jesus' full salvation. The word *salvation*, used so much in the New Testament, really means wholeness. God wants wholeness for people. He wants us whole and healthy—mentally, spiritually, socially—in all that we are as a unified personality. Christ's salvation permeates our entire personhood just as in the case of the healed woman. Again, this does not mean every believer will be healthy, wealthy and a celebrity. It does mean that God will touch every area of life and grant what is best for us. Therefore, if our witness is to be effective, we must minister to the total person.

Simply expressed, real ministry does not deal only with spiritual things; it gets into the blood, sweat, and tears of human needs. Furthermore, in all holistic ministry, no partiality can be allowed (James 2:1-7). The church must exclude no one. God's people are to cross all racial, economic, cultural, and human barriers to meet needs. That presents a serious challenge. We often have hangups and preconceived ideas about certain people and situations. That is why James urges us to love—regardless of who the person is (James 2:1-9). Love moves into any life. Love attempts to meet every need of anyone regardless of any man-made category that would separate people.

Now all this never implies that spiritual needs should be relegated to a secondary role. To the contrary, spiritual needs always arise as paramount. As one put it, "To love as Jesus loved is to see what he sees, the soul's needs, the eternal interests."[7] A person stands in need, desperate for salvation from sin more than he or she needs anything else. It was D. L. Moody who said, "There is no greater honor than to be the instrument in God's hands of leading one person out of the kingdom of Satan into the glorious light of heaven." And every believer who loves can be just such an instrument. But simply because spiritual needs always stand as primary, this does not discharge us from meeting social and physical needs. Further, often people will not open up to our spiritual ministry of witness if we ignore these temporal problems. A hungry man has no ears.

Our society finds itself increasingly secular. We may have to spend some time helping these so-called postmodern people understand the whole worldview of the Scriptures. There are so many different understandings today of God, sin, spirituality, salvation, eternity, and so forth, that taking time with the secularists to help them grasp the worldview of the Bible becomes vital. Only as one grasps what the Scriptures present as the course of God's dealings—biblical history in the broad sense—does the gospel itself make sense. This calls for establishing loving relationships and sacrificially taking time with people in helping them to Christ. Remember that Peter said,

"Sanctify Christ as Lord in your hearts, always being ready to make a defense to everyone who asks you to give an account for the hope that is in you, yet with gentleness and reverence" (1 Peter 3:15).

Our whole approach must be to start with people where we find them and be sensitive to what they feel as needful in their lives. Then we work patiently and lovingly and understandingly with them until they see the need for Christ. That may take time. It surely takes our creating a healthy relationship. *It will surely take love.* But this approach gives the church real power in its witness. And after all, that is what Jesus did.

But we do have something definite to say. We do have a specific word of witness to share—and it is a message of power (Rom. 1:16).

The Word of Witness

What is this gospel to which we give witness? The Scripture that tells us can be found in Acts 2:22-24. Acts 2 records the message given on the Day of Pentecost. In that setting, Peter preached these penetrating words:

> Men of Israel, listen to these words: Jesus the Nazarene, a man attested to you by God with miracles and wonders and signs which God performed through Him in your midst, just as you yourselves know—this Man, delivered up by the predetermined plan and foreknowledge of God, you nailed to a cross by the hands of godless men and put Him to death. And God raised Him up again, putting an end to the agony of death, since it was impossible for Him to be held in its power.

This constitutes the heart of the gospel because it outlines the heart of the entire Christ-event. It speaks of our Lord's incarnation—Jesus was "a man." It tells us that He lived a magnificent life, revealing God. Further, it all centers in the Lord's sacrificial death for our sins and the glorious resurrection, victory over sin, death, hell, the demons and the devil and the world. That presents a powerful message. As Luke recorded Peter's gospel message, he tells us in verse 37 of Acts 2, "Now when they [the hearers] heard this [the gospel], they were pierced to the heart, and said to Peter and the rest of the apostles, 'Brethren, what shall we do?'" Peter replied, "Repent, and let each of you be baptized in the name of Jesus Christ for the forgiveness of your sins; and you shall receive the gift of the Holy Spirit" (Acts 2:38). The call to repentance and faith completes the basic gospel appeal. When people realize God's great love and their deep need of forgiveness of sins—because it was their (and our) sins that nailed Him to the cross—the Holy Spirit uses this and "cuts to the heart." As the seeking soul raises the question, "What must we do?" Paul puts it all together when he said to the Ephesian elders, "repentance toward God and faith in our Lord Jesus Christ" (Acts 20:21). This entire message brings people to living faith in Jesus Christ; this is the powerful gospel (Rom. 1:16).

Therefore, the message that we must share as the Holy Spirit leads and gives opportunity is the message of Christ. We don't talk primarily about our church, our pastor, or this or that secondary matter. Those things are important, but what brings people to the Lord centers in the hearing of the gospel. We must never forget that Jesus said, "You shall be *My* witnesses" (Acts 1:8).

Several New Testament scholars have built on this basic Pentecost sermon and put in a systematic fashion the truths that the apostles shared to bring others to Christ. Along with the Acts chapter two passage, students of the Word also take up Paul's statement in 1 Corinthians 1:21: "For since in the wisdom of God the world through its wisdom did not come to know God, God was well-pleased through the foolishness of

the *message preached [kerygma]* to save those who believe"
(emphasis added). The key Greek word in this verse,
kerygma, can be best translated "what we preach." Paul said
that the Holy Spirit uses the "preached word" as His sword to
bring others to Jesus, even if they call it "folly." Hence we
should fully understand the meaning of kerygma if we aspire
to be an effective, loving witness for Christ. Actually, the word
is a synonym for gospel (Rom. 1:16). To understand the
content of the kerygma, the proclamation of the gospel,
guarantees God's blessings of power.

Michael Green, New Testament scholar, presents three
essential truths that center around the meaning of the gospel
or the proclamation (kerygma). First, the apostles preached a
Person. Their message was frankly and unapologetically
Christocentric. The Good News of Jesus centered on His
matchless life and public ministry. But the central emphasis
pointed to His death and glorious resurrection.

Green holds, in the second place, that the early church
proclaimed a gift. God offers the gift of forgiveness, the gift of
the Holy Spirit, the gift of adoption and reconciliation. That kind
of grace made "no people" the "people of God." Concerning
the idea of a gift, the emphasis rested on the gift of forgiveness
and the gift of the Holy Spirit in apostolic proclamation.

Third, the first-century church looked for a response from
her hearers. The apostles were anything but shy in asking people
to decide then and there for or against Christ. They expected
results—positive results. These early witnesses declared that
all seekers must do three things in the light of the gospel: (1)
They must repent. This surfaced as first and foremost in the
declaration. (2) They must exercise faith. This means a
continuing life of faith, although it certainly begins by a "leap
of faith." Moreover, true faith can never be divorced from
repentance. They make up two sides of the same coin. (3) The
apostles declared baptism. The rite became the seal on God's

offer of forgiveness and the essence of our response to that offer in repentance and faith.[8]

The evangelical church, by and large, views baptism as an act of obedience in professing openly the grace of salvation that repentance and faith bring.

Another interesting writer on the theme of proclaiming Christ is James Stewart. He set forth his ideas in his helpful book, *A Faith to Proclaim*. He asks:

> What, then, was the essence of this proclamation by the original heralds of the faith? Quite briefly it was this. They proclaimed that prophecy was fulfilled; that in Jesus of Nazareth, in His words and deeds, His life and death and resurrection, the new age had arrived; that God had exalted Him, that He would come again as Judge, and that now was the day of salvation. This was the message.[9]

Stewart derives five principles that should be found in all gospel witnessing and proclamation. To begin with, the witness must declare the *incarnation*. The facts of the gospel are historical and unique. The doctrine of the incarnation means that "God has come right into the midst of the tumult and the shouting of this world."[10] The kingdom of God, no less, has broken into the here and now. That will always remain unique and unrepeatable.

The faithful evangelist and witness also proclaims *forgiveness*. How relevant, for "wherever the Church truly proclaims the forgiveness of sins there the healing ministry is veritably at work."[11] The meaninglessness and lack of direction in life, seen everywhere in our secular society, should be recognized as a problem of sin. Iniquity and rebellion against God lurk as the ultimate culprits in the contemporary loss of identity and feeling of aloneness. As the church preaches forgiveness, it strikes right at the heart of many present-day problems. Kierkegaard said, "I must repent myself back into the family, into the clan, into the race, back to God."[12]

In the third place, Stewart states that the proclaimer tells the story of the Cross. The veil of the temple has been rent, the veil that kept men out of God's presence and that shut God in. The darkness and mystery of God's "Holy otherness" has now been flung open. Reality can be touched. As Stewart expresses it: "The death of Christ gives me the very heart of the eternal, because it is not words at all, not even sublime prophetic utterance: It is an act, God's act, against which I can batter all my doubts to pieces. We preach Christ crucified, God's truth revealed."[13] The Cross speaks of atonement, guilt-bearing, and reconciliation. Moreover, the demonic forces of the universe were once and for all defeated. Christ has overcome the world. He conquered. What love! What power! What victory! "We preach Christ crucified" always becomes the cry of the evangelistic witness.

Fourth, the "hour cometh, and now is." The new age, the long-expected hope, has arrived. Christ has been raised. We declare a resurrected, living Lord. "This is indeed the very core of the apostolic (message)."[14] Every early Christian sermon and word of witness gladly proclaimed this glorious fact.

The resurrection forms no mere appendix to the message, merely tacked on the end of our witness. The resurrection became a cosmic event. All history was shattered by this creative act of God almighty. Nothing can ever be the same again. Therefore, the apostolic message never presented Good Friday and Easter as two isolated events. The early believers always declared them as one mighty stroke of God. Time has now been baptized into eternity; things on this side immersed in things on the other. There is no atonement and reconciliation apart from the resurrection. God's act of justification has been revealed. "This is our gospel. For this is what Christianity essentially is—a religion of Resurrection."[15]

In summary, Stewart declares that the witness simply shares

Christ. The message is not a cold, conceptualized theology or philosophy. A person is presented, a person in love sent to us. And what a person He is—Helper, Shepherd, Companion, Friend, Light, Bread of Life, *Paraclete*. If Christianity is anything, it is an experience of a "vital relationship to a living Christ."[16] How the world needs to make this great discovery! How different contemporary society would become if people truly understood what all this means! Love will send us to them to tell them.

The proclamation, the glorious gospel of God's love, can be best summarized from Peter's sermon on the Day of Pentecost (Acts 2). He declared:

- ❧ The new-age has arrived in Jesus Christ (2:16-21, 36).
- ❧ The life of Christ is proclaimed (2:22).
- ❧ The death of Christ is declared (2:23, 36).
- ❧ The resurrection of Christ is announced (2:24, 31-32).
- ❧ The return of Christ is shared (2:35).
- ❧ The call to repentance and faith is set forth (2:38).
- ❧ The promise of the gift of forgiveness and the Holy Spirit is given (2:33).

Therefore, this becomes the message to share in every way possible. God's Holy Spirit employs it to convict and convert. Nothing else has that power. As Paul put it, "I am not ashamed of the gospel: it is the power of God for salvation to every one who has faith, to the Jew first and also to the Greek" (Rom. 1:16 rsv). We need to communicate it simply and effectively. Most of us need some practical help on that score, however. So to a simple, workable approach to witnessing we finally turn.

A Method in Witnessing to the Whole Person

A simple formula in witnessing for Christ may prove helpful in expressing our love for Christ. It can often overcome the difficulty of beginning a presentation of the gospel. That hurdle often seems a high one to clear.

Realize, of course, that there may be much background work in relation building, loving ministry, putting the truth in sensible terms so the secular mind can grasp it. But then we can proceed in sharing the gospel in simple step-by-step fashion.

The first step normally starts off with some sort of secular talk. Rarely should our first words to one with whom we hope to share Christ be, "Are you saved, brother?" or some such expression. That puts most people off today. Usually the best start begins with people's interest in the secular sense; for example, being friendly, gracious, complimentary, and courteous. This is wise and can help establish rapport. It may be a period of time before one can go on to more spiritual matters. As emphasized, establishing a real relationship with the person may prove vital. That can be costly, but love never asks, "Who is my neighbor?" Rather, it asks, "How can I be neighborly?" Love demands such sacrifices. No one is won easily. Henry Drummond set a beautiful example here.

Next, we can in most instances engage them in "church talk." Tell about what the church means to you. From secular talk to church talk does not require a big leap. Of course one does not stop there. We really haven't witnessed if we restrict ourselves to church talk only. The gospel is the word of witness, and the gospel does not center in the church. Still, it can begin to open the door to more spiritual matters.

Then the door may be opened to share one's testimony. Ask, for example, "Do you know why I enjoy church?" Then share your faith. Tell them what Christ means to you personally. Paul loved sharing his testimony and did so on every occasion, even before kings (Acts 26). One may get no further than this at any certain stage. But moving toward the goal of a full gospel witness is the point.

Finally, ask something like, "Would you desire to know how

Jesus Christ can do for you what He has done for me?" Surprisingly, a number of people will say "yes." Then you can share the full message of Jesus Christ. You can in love challenge them to receive Christ. Lead them in prayer. That is witnessing.

The wisdom of such a rudimentary four-step presentation becomes obvious. It moves along naturally and presents a systematic and simple way to share Christ. One step merges into the next. One does not come on strong like a "hot gospel buttonholer." That approach rarely wins the lost—especially today. If you have had difficulty getting into a conversation about Christ, this method may be used by God—even if it takes a minute or a month or a year to get to the gospel. Simply keep the goal in mind.

Two cautions need be made, however. You must lead the conversation. You must keep on track and get to the gospel as the Holy Spirit leads, whether it takes a long or short time. Jesus did this in talking to the Samaritan woman at Jacob's well (John 4). She tried to sidetrack the Lord on secondary issues, but Jesus kept her need always before her. He kept bringing her back to the real issue. This does not mean that you are rude or refuse to answer honest questions. Dialogue is essential. And we need to have ready answers. Recall what Peter told us, "But sanctify Christ as Lord in your hearts, always being ready to make a defense to everyone who asks you to give an account for the hope that is in you" (1 Peter 3:15a). We should make the sacrifice of love to study so that we do have answers for honest seekers. This is part of agape also.

Furthermore, the witnessing must be kept very personal. Help the person see his or her need—personally. Make Jesus alive. You are not presenting a theological dissertation; a person stands at the core of our conversation. Remember, the gospel has not been fully presented until a person receives the challenge to repent of sins and believe in Jesus. Give the conditions of salvation as well as the Christ of salvation. And let us *never* forget, if the person to whom we share the gospel responds, we must help them to begin the nurturing process of getting into a church, learning the disciplines of discipleship and service, and growing in grace (2 Peter 3:18).

But in the final analysis, we learn to witness by doing it. No more than you can learn to fly an airplane by reading a book on aerodynamics, do you learn to witness by studying a book. You must do it. As we love people and try to meet their needs, we learn to share Christ, and effective witnessing wins. It may well be that God will use you to help others encounter the greatest thing in the world—God's unfathomable love. One thing cannot be refuted; if we truly love people as God loves them, we will be compelled to witness to God's great love in Christ. Love serves.

Conclusion

One final summary statement seems appropriate: The degree of our love for God and for a suffering world can be measured only by the depth of our dedication to step into needy lives and meet those needs. We must never forget, as Paul said, that "the love of Christ controls us." Real agape love truly does serve, just as it obeys and bears fruit. What a wonderful work the grace of God, through the inner action of the Holy Spirit, has accomplished in the life of every believer in Jesus Christ. Now we can truly and deeply love God and our neighbors. That makes life worth living.

Thank you, Henry Drummond, for reminding us what true love is. You were right—it is the greatest thing in the world.

Endnotes

1. John R. W. Stott, *Our Guilty Silence* (London: Hodder and Stoughton, 1967), 25.
2. John R. W. Stott, *One People* (London: Falcon Books, 1969), 24.
3. Marcus Dods, *The First Epistle to the Corinthians*; The Expositors Bible (London: Hodder and Stoughton, 1891), 276.

4. Archibald Robertson and Alfred Plummer, *A Critical and Exegetical Commentary on the First Epistle of St. Paul to the Corinthians,* The International Critical Commentary (Edinburgh: T. & T. Clark, 1953), 264.

5. Alexander Rattray Haye, *The New Testament Order for Church and Missionary* (New Testament Missionary Union, 1947), 177.

6. William Barclay, *The Letter to the Corinthians,* (Edinburgh: St. Andrews Press, 1954), 124.

7. R. C. H. Lenski, *The Interpretation of St. John's Gospel* (Minneapolis: Augsburg, 1963), 1048.

8. Michael Green, *Evangelism in the Early Church* (London: Hodder and Stoughton, 1970), 150-52.

9. James S. Stewart, *A Faith to Proclaim* (New York: Charles Scribner Sons, 1953), 14-15.

10. Ibid., 18.

11. Ibid., 50.

12. Ibid., 55.

13. Ibid., 82.

14. Ibid., 104.

15. Ibid., 110.

16. Ibid., 143.

Epilogue

A fitting epitaph to the life, ministry, and impact of Henry Drummond was expressed by biographer James W. Kennedy when he wrote:

There are many memorials erected in loving memory of Henry Drummond. A beautiful drinking fountain was given to the City of Glasgow and placed in the West End Park by Lord and Lady Aberdeen on the fifth anniversary of his death. Affixed to the pillar is a profile bust of Drummond circled by a laurel wreath, executed in bronze by the distinguished King's sculptor for Scotland, James Pittendrigh Macfillivray, R.S.A. Around the head is his name. Underneath is the inscription of the text used to welcome the Aberdeen family to Quebec in 1893. "There is a river, the streams whereof make glad the city of God." On the other side of the pillar is a bronze tablet with the inscription "1851 H.D. 1897." A copy of this same plaque is in the ante-chapel of Haddo House with another inscription underneath: "In memory of Henry Drummond and the message he gave in this place." The bas-relief is flanked on either side by the texts of the first and last sermons he preached in that chapel. There is another replica placed in the Governor's Residence in

Quebec. There is still another copy, mounted on white marble and placed on the second floor of Trinity College, Glasgow, at the end of the hall opposite the stairs. The first two replicas were given by Lord and Lady Aberdeen, while the third one was given by Henry's oldest brother, James, in 1903. There is a stained-glass window on the stair landing in the foyer of Trinity College, given in memory of Professors James Smith Candlish and Henry Drummond by students and friends. The Possilpark Church, where he did such an important work, is now named the Henry Drummond (Memorial) Parish Church of the Church of Scotland.

Henry Drummond's greatest memorial, however, is a living one—his effect upon human lives by confronting them with Jesus Christ. The testimonials are endless of Drummond's life-changing and regenerating influence on others. From the most famous down to the least significant come words which tell of his abiding influence on the thinking and living of all who heard him or read his writings. One such testimony is typical: "I owe more to him than I do any other mortal." His influence still abides in his word; and, even though we can never have the same wonderful privilege of standing in his bright and exhilarating presence, accorded those fortunate ones of his era, we can still feel the power of life through his word, which breathed the very spirit of the Christ who was Henry Drummond's Master and Lord. For he lived at the center of his religion.[1]

So the memory of Henry Drummond—brilliant professor, scintillating preacher, able witness to the gospel, man of God, a sterling example of Christian love—lingers on. After one hundred years, his life and ministry to the glory of God remains deeply appreciated, and continues to be used by the Holy Spirit.

When Drummond discovered that the greatest thing in the world was love, and then attempted to live his life in that setting, it became inevitable that he would make a lasting impression for the glory of Jesus Christ. This author trusts that it has made a lasting impression on the reader for God's glory and honor. May multitudes, past and present and future, impacted by his grasp of the essence of Christian love, rise to the challenge he presented. May God raise up many who will follow his lead and love even as Christ has loved us.

Endnotes

1. James W. Kennedy, *Henry Drummond: An Anthology* (New York: Harper and Brothers Publishers, 1953), 61-62.